BEST RADIO
PLAYS OF 1985

Previous Giles Cooper Award volumes

Pearl by John Arden (Special Award 1978)

Best Radio Plays of 1978
Richard Harris: *Is It Something I Said?*
Don Haworth: *Episode on a Thursday Evening*
Jill Hyem: *Remember Me*
Tom Mallin: *Halt! Who Goes There?*
Jennifer Phillips: *Daughters of Men*
Fay Weldon: *Polaris*

Best Radio Plays of 1979
Shirley Gee: *Typhoid Mary*
Carey Harrison: *I Never Killed My German*
Barrie Keeffe: *Heaven Scent*
John Kirkmorris: *Coxcomb*
John Peacock: *Attard in Retirement*
Olwen Wymark: *The Child*

Best Radio Plays of 1980
Stewart Parker: *The Kamikaze Groundstaff Reunion Dinner*
Martyn Read: *Waving to a Train*
Peter Redgrove: *Martyr of the Hives*
William Trevor: *Beyond the Pale*

Best Radio Plays of 1981
Peter Barnes: *The Jumping Mimuses of Byzantium*
Don Haworth: *Talk of Love and War*
Harold Pinter: *Family Voices*
David Pownall: *Beef*
J.P. Rooney: *The Dead Image*
Paul Thain: *The Biggest Sandcastle in the World*

Best Radio Plays of 1982
Rhys Adrian: *Watching the Plays Together*
John Arden: *The Old Man Sleeps Alone*
Harry Barton: *Hoopoe Day*
Donald Chapman: *Invisible Writing*
Tom Stoppard: *The Dog It Was That Died*
William Trevor: *Autumn Sunshine*

Best Radio Plays of 1983
Wally K. Daly: *Time Slip*
Shirley Gee: *Never In My Lifetime*
Gerry Jones: *The Angels They Grow Lonely*
Steve May: *No Exceptions*
Martyn Read: *Scouting for Boys*

Best Radio Plays of 1984
Stephen Dunstone: *Who Is Sylvia?*
Robert Ferguson: *Transfigured Night*
Don Haworth: *Daybreak*
Caryl Phillips: *The Wasted Years*
Christopher Russell: *Swimmer*
Rose Tremain: *Temporary Shelter*

BEST RADIO PLAYS OF 1985

The Giles Cooper Award Winners

Rhys Adrian: Outpatient
Barry Collins: King Canute
Martin Crimp: Three Attempted Acts
David Pownall: Ploughboy Monday
James Saunders: Menocchio
Michael Wall: Hiroshima: The Movie

METHUEN/ BBC PUBLICATIONS

First published in Great Britain in 1986 by Methuen London Ltd,
11 New Fetter Lane, London EC4P 4EE and in the United States of
America by Methuen Inc, 29 West 35th Street, New York, NY 10001,
and BBC Publications, 35 Marylebone High Street, London W1M 4AA.

Set in IBM 10 point Journal by Words & Pictures Limited,
Thornton Heath, Surrey

Printed and bound in Great Britain

British Library Cataloguing in Publication Data

Best radio plays of . . .
   1985
   1. Radio plays, English—Periodicals
   822'.02'08   PR1259.R33
   ISBN 0-413-41640-2

CONTENTS

Page

Note on the selection   vi

Preface   vii

OUTPATIENT   1

KING CANUTE   19

THREE ATTEMPTED ACTS   51

PLOUGHBOY MONDAY   81

MENOCCHIO   125

HIROSHIMA: THE MOVIE   143

THE GILES COOPER AWARDS: a note on the selection

Giles Cooper

As one of the most original and inventive radio playwrights of the post-war years, Giles Cooper was the author who came most clearly to mind when the BBC and Methuen were in search of a name when first setting up their jointly sponsored radio drama awards in 1978. Particularly so, as the aim of the awards is precisely to encourage original radio writing by both new and established authors — encouragement in the form of both public acclaim and of publication of their work in book form.

Eligibility

Eligible for the awards was every original radio play first broadcast by the BBC domestic service from December 1984 to December 1985 (almost 500 plays in total). Excluded·from consideration were translations, adaptations and dramatised 'features'. In order to ensure that the broad range of radio playwriting was represented, the judges aimed to select plays which offered a variety of length, subject matter and technique by authors with differing experience of writing for radio.

Selection

The producers-in-charge of the various drama 'slots' were each asked to put forward about five or six plays for the judges' consideration. This resulted in a 'short-list' of some 30 plays from which the final selection was made. The judges were entitled to nominate further plays for consideration provided they were eligible. Selection was made on the strength of the script rather than of the production, since it was felt that the awards were primarily for writing and that production could unduly enhance or detract from the merits of the original script.

Judges

The judges for the 1985 awards were:
> Susanna Capon, who formerly worked in radio, and is now an independent television producer
> Nicholas Hern, Drama Editor, Methuen London
> Richard Imison, Script Editor, BBC Radio Drama
> B.A. Young, who was formerly the *Financial Times* drama critic, and who now writes on radio for the same paper

PREFACE

It was about twenty years ago, I recall, somewhere in the mid 1960s, that a mild sport of television planning decreed that the characters from one of the fashionable serials of the time should appear briefly in the storyline of one of the others. To be honest, I can't now remember which two serials were involved, though I'm fairly certain that they were unrelated (in style as well as content) rather than simply first cousins like *Z Cars* and *Softly Softly*. At all events, the idea was quite amusing and indeed prompted memories of an even earlier occasion, in the late forties, when on radio members of the Robinson family (the 'Front Line Family' of the war years) paid a courtesy call on the Wimbledon home of the upstart Mrs Dale; a gesture designed, I'm sure, to pass on the baton of familiarity, to the new (and, it was to be hoped, long distance) runner.

Amusement at television's family joke was followed quickly by a somewhat less agreeable thought: suppose that the long-running serial, or soap-opera, was indeed a form with which the audience identified so closely that it became not mere entertainment but a substitute reality? There was evidence for this in radio's long experience of *The Archers* and *Mrs Dale's Diary*. The tragic death of Grace Archer in a fire on 22 September 1955 — the very night that commercial television launched its service to the nation — was not simply taken as a piece of astute planning on the part of the BBC in the face of competition but as a reason for widespread mourning. Listeners felt a sense of personal loss, even of grief, and when the 'funeral' took place Broadcasting House received a number of wreaths. Other examples of over-identification were quite common in radio serials. Might not the phenomenon be even more marked in television? And might the use of one serial (rather than a real person) to provide a testimonial, as it were, to another, presage a development in which pseudo-reality became preferable to untreated fact? Perhaps soap-operas would be born and intermarry to the point where television became one continuous family saga, in which the viewer would see such obligatory flashes of reality such as the news bulletins not directly on their own sets but on the set of the fictional family in the story they were watching.

In the 1960s, such a fantasy of the future was entertaining but perhaps just a shade baroque. *Dynasty II: The Colbys* was still a long way off, and I think no one would seriously have anticipated the situation recently reported in the press of American viewers jamming the switchboards with protests because coverage of the space shuttle disaster was interrupting their favourite 'soaps'.

The long-running serials have, I believe, more in common than might at first appear. Despite the apparent range of style and subject matter — from farming in the Midlands to oil-rich mayhem in the American West; from daily life in the industrial north or the problems of hotel-keeping, to the glitter and glamour of tinsel city itself — the soap opera depends for its success on the very predictability of its plot and characters. It is comforting to find that the head of an oil empire doesn't live in misanthropic isolation, obsessed with the mysteries of the stock market and preoccupied with the absorbing (but essentially undramatic) minutiae involved in the activity of making unimaginably large sums of money grow even unimaginably larger; but is after all exactly like us, pettily tottering from day to day, concerned with the all-too-recognisable problems of survival, spiced occasionally with pleasurable speculation about who sleeps with whom.

It is also encouraging to find that behind the harsh realities of unemployment and recession in the north of England, community life seems to carry on relatively unimpeded. Whatever admirable concerns are expressed in the course of twice-weekly conversation, it is no accident that so prominent a part of *Coronation Street* takes place in the comforting atmosphere of The Rover's Return. However individual, inventive and socially aware the storylines of soap opera may sometimes be, one cannot escape either the practical mechanics or the attendant publicity paraphernalia which combine to create an atmosphere of conformity and reassurance. The fact that both people and places reappear regularly is at the very heart of the long-running serial's appeal.

That's fine, and no one would deny to the audience something which it so manifestly enjoys but it does also lead to the thought that in spite of their superficial similarity at the point of consumption, the soap opera and the single play actually have very little in common; and, moreover, that the striking divergence between radio and television in the matter of serials and single plays results from something even more fundamental than the great difference in cost of drama in the two media.

In the eight years since the first of these volumes appeared, two things have characterised the output of the BBC's Radio Drama Department more than all else, and have separated it not only from television but from what has become the norm of radio drama in many parts of the world. The two things are the sheer quantity of output — of which I have written in earlier volumes — and the range of single plays which are included in our concept of true radio drama. I believe that the two go closely hand in hand.

One of the great joys of radio drama is its capacity to encompass a variety of different forms: the monologue, the conventional narrative, the verse play, the epic, the musical, the abstract composition of words and sounds — all have a legitimate place in radio's theatre of the mind's eye. In Britain at least it is of importance that popular plays share air time with works of greater literary pretension — and that the former are not categorised separately (as they are in some other European countries) as 'entertainment' programmes rather than drama proper. In our view, good drama should be entertaining; and what truly entertains can make good drama and needs no apology.

What links these diverse forms legitimately under the one heading of radio drama is a quality which is the antithesis of that which assures the popularity of the soap opera. It is a quality of novelty rather than familiarity; it flourishes out of the unknown or the unexpected; it informs and extends and stimulates; at its best, it educates in the wide, satisfying sense of the founding BBC doctrine. It is dedicated not so much to giving the audience what it wants as to providing an experience which much of the audience had never previously conceived. When the single play becomes predictable and reassuring, it becomes (unlike the serial) that much less satisfactory.

Of course, stimulation on this scale is a tall order, and would be so even given far larger resources than BBC Radio possesses and an inexhaustible supply of outstanding talent. In practice, the net is cast wide to bring in a range of skill and knowledge, from the most experienced writers to those who are only just finding their feet in this medium of daunting opportunity. The plays which result are therefore sometimes gripping, sometimes hesitant. They travel throughout the world and through time. They amuse, or move or hold in suspense. Sometimes they shock, or stir to indignation or anger. They deal with noble emotions and base instincts; with inspiring poetry and with crudity and violence — for all of those exist in the range of human experience with which drama is concerned.

Perhaps too often the radio play merely achieves a competence: a reasonably interesting story reasonably well told and performed. I sometimes think that that's when radio drama is nearest to failure — nearer than when it attempts something strange and difficult and baffles many who hear it. For our single fictions should be as strange as truth and at least as gripping; our oil millionaires curiously revealing why it is that we are *not* of their number, rather than making us wonder how they rose undeservedly to riches. King Lear has no need to visit Rookery Nook, and life should continue to fascinate in its complexity. To that concept of the single play we continue to dedicate our efforts.

Richard Imison
(February 1986)

OUTPATIENT

by Rhys Adrian

For Mavis and for John

Rhys Adrian was born in London and lives and works in Chiswick. He was a stage manager for summer shows, revues, pantomimes and West End musicals before becoming a full-time writer. He is married to the dancer Mavis Traill and has two sons.

Outpatient was first broadcast on BBC Radio 3 on 8 May 1985. The cast was as follows:

EDWARD	Michael Aldridge
MARTIN	Andrew Sachs
WOMAN	Sylvia Coleridge
NURSE	Margot Boyd

Director: John Tydeman
Running time, as broadcast: 33 minutes 12 seconds.

MARTIN *sits with a groan and a grunt. Pause. Another groan and grunt.*

EDWARD. My dear fellow, are you feeling all right?

MARTIN. There is nothing to me at all. I should be at least two stone heavier than I am. The weight just slipped away. Overnight. Well, almost. That was why I was sent here in the first place. But no nearer the truth. No nearer discovery. I am as light as a feather, but when I visit this place my legs can barely support me. I seem to weigh a ton.

EDWARD. No nearer the truth in my case either. No nearer discovery.

MARTIN. Have I seen you here before?

EDWARD. I seem to have seen you here before. But this is the first time we have sat together. Or spoken to each other.

MARTIN. That is because the only seat that is vacant is the one nearest to you. That sounded offensive. I didn't mean to be offensive to you.

A tinny voice comes over the tannoy.

VOICE (*we can only just make out what is being said*). Would Mr Johnson please go to consulting room number six.

MARTIN. Who do they want?

EDWARD. No idea. Infernal machine. There is a click. A pause. Then a cracked voice summoning someone to go somewhere. It is not even possible to see where they have hidden the speaker. Behind that metal grille? That metal grille? Behind the cupboard. Or even inside the cupboard. I ignore it. I always wait for the nurse to come and call me in person. And where, in any case, would room number six be? Up or down which corridor? The place is like a maze. Some of the doors are numbered. Some are not. I sometimes think the signs on the walls are meant to confuse you. That by the time you eventually get to see the doctor you are so thoroughly confused that whatever he says goes right over the top of your head.

WOMAN. Excuse me.

MARTIN. Yes?

WOMAN. But was that for me?

MARTIN. Was what for you?

WOMAN. The call. They called for someone. Over the speaker.

MARTIN. Take no notice of it.

WOMAN. But I must.

MARTIN. Why?

WOMAN. I don't know where I am.

EDWARD. Are you sure you're in the right clinic, madam?

WOMAN. I never know.

EDWARD. Are you sure you're in the right hospital?

WOMAN. Of course I am.

EDWARD. I never know if I am or not. We are now sitting in the annexe. When I was last here there was no annexe. A different receptionist. A different part of the hospital. But my file always seems to be here when I arrive. So I always think, not too senile yet. Not written off quite just yet. A little bit of the spark still remaining. Not quite snuffed out yet.

WOMAN. The call must have been for someone. But no one has moved.

MARTIN. It wouldn't have been for me. I've only just got here.

WOMAN. But it must have been for someone.

MARTIN. I wouldn't know if it was for you or not, madam. I don't even know who you are.

WOMAN. I've seen you here before.

MARTIN. I've seen you here before, too. But I don't know your name. Who do you have to see?

WOMAN. Mr Robinson. Today. That's what they said.

MARTIN. I have to see him too. Then we must suffer from the same complaint. Whatever it is. No one seems too sure. No one's absolutely clear. Did you suffer from a sudden loss of weight?

WOMAN. How did you know that?

MARTIN. It seems that's his speciality. Whatever his speciality is. It is all frightfully morbid to me. Are you here to see Mr Robinson?

EDWARD. Not absolutely sure. They pricked the end of my finger. A sample of blood. Usual ghastly business with the urine. Then I was told to wait in here.

MARTIN. Did they weigh you?

EDWARD. They always do.

WOMAN. Why should you know my name?

MARTIN. There is no reason in the world why I should, madam.

WOMAN. I've been here almost an hour.

MARTIN. It's no good complaining to me. There is nothing I can do about it. I have to be as patient as everyone else. I am as much at the mercy of the system as you are yourself, madam.

EDWARD. I have been here a little over two hours.

MARTIN. Madam. Go back to your seat. If no one goes in answer to the tannoy, then Nurse will have to come.

WOMAN. You want me to go to my seat?

MARTIN. I don't *want* you to do anything. All I want to do is to sit here quietly and contemplate my predicament. Whatever it may be. My problem is that no one has told me what my predicament really is. Or if they have, I have forgotten. It is a month since I was last here. A lot of probing questions. Some too sensitive to even give an answer to. I will never answer anything to do with my innards.

EDWARD. I am extremely sensitive on that point too.

MARTIN. There. Look. Someone has risen.

EDWARD. From the grave, it looks like, too. Still alive. He looks as though he should have been dead years ago. Hardly walk. Tapping the way up the corridor with his stick. Not really knowing where he is going. He'll never get there.

WOMAN. Where?

EDWARD. To wherever it is he is going.

MARTIN. Madam. Please take your seat. If you don't go when you are called, then Nurse will come and fetch you.

WOMAN. I am to go to my seat?

MARTIN. Please.
The corridors are lined with people. No one really feeling anything. All of them. Staring into space, most of them. The infernal wait.

EDWARD. I always bring a book with me. But I never manage to read it.

WOMAN. I don't really want to be here at all.

MARTIN. None of us want to be here, madam. But we are required to be here. For our own good. So they tell us.

WOMAN. But I have so many things to do. A whole morning here?

EDWARD. Sometimes a whole day. I once arrived at nine-thirty one morning and wasn't seen until four-thirty that afternoon. I sometimes think that a week might pass before I am finally seen. That I might arrive on a Monday and leave on a Friday, the weekend off, then back on Monday to continue the wait. Nil by mouth in all that time.

MARTIN. Purgatory.

EDWARD. And leaving at the end of it none the wiser for it all. A thousand samples of blood. A thousand specimens of urine. The infernal queue. The one urinal.

MARTIN. Purgatory.

Pause.

Please sit down, madam. You will rest your legs.

WOMAN. If you hear them call for Mrs Jenkins, you'll be sure to tell me.

MARTIN. Please return to your seat.

WOMAN. You want me to return to my seat, then?

MARTIN. Please, madam. I am not myself today. I feel incredibly old.

EDWARD (*sotto*). Here comes Nurse.

MARTIN. Not looking too pleased, by the look of it.

NURSE. Has anyone here seen Mr Jones?

EDWARD. Mr Jones, Nurse?

NURSE. He was sitting near to you. A white-haired man with dark glasses.

EDWARD. I don't recall a white-haired man. Not sitting next to me.

NURSE. We sent him for a urine sample two hours ago. He hasn't been seen since.

EDWARD (*softly*). Perhaps he's escaped.

MARTIN (*softly*). Perhaps he tunnelled his way out.

EDWARD (*softly*). Over the wall.

MARTIN (*softly*). To freedom.

NURSE. Oh, dear. Has no one seen Mr Jones?

ALL. No, Nurse.

NURSE (*going*). Oh, dear, oh, dear. Where can he be?

Pause.

EDWARD. I, too, feel the years piling on when I arrive at the hospital. You don't see the building until you turn the bend in the road. And, then, there it is. I always hope, that one day, when I turn that bend, I will find the place demolished. Yet at the end of it. When I am released back into the outside world, I feel the years slipping away again. I then go and do all the things I shouldn't do. I go to a bar. There is a nice bar up the road. Quiet.

MARTIN. I know it.

EDWARD. I have several beers. Followed by several whiskies. Full of outpatients, of course. Mulling over their respective fates. Brooding over their drinks. Trying to remember what has just been said to them. I celebrate my freedom yet again. I am my own master again for another month. Take the tablets when you feel like it. Take the tablets when you can possibly remember. Test the urine after the main meal, hoping for the stick to turn blue, a negative response, but watching it turn green. No cause for alarm there. Not too positive a colour. And another whisky. The colour of the stick known only to me. No one to admonish me. I never admonish myself. I wouldn't see the point in doing so. I stand in front of the mirror and raise my glass to myself. Another day! To, somehow, have got through another day!

VOICE (*on the tannoy*). Would Mr Morrison please go to consulting room number three.

WOMAN. Me? Jenkins?

MARTIN. No, madam. Not Jenkins. Morrison, as far as I could tell.

EDWARD. See who goes. A skeleton.

MARTIN. But still a spark of life to him.

EDWARD. A residue.

Pause.

Someone keeled over. When I was here. Last month.

MARTIN. I was here. I was sitting on the other side of the room.

EDWARD. Everyone feeling too awkward to do anything about it. Everyone looking away.

MARTIN. I didn't know what to do. I didn't know where to look.

EDWARD. Eventually I went and called Nurse.

MARTIN. I remember you going for the nurse.

EDWARD. A lot of thumping of the chest went on.

MARTIN. I remember the thumping of the chest.

EDWARD. Then in they came with the resuscitation trolley.

MARTIN. I remember them rushing in with that.

EDWARD. Hopeless, of course. Then the orderlies coming in with the stretcher.

MARTIN. I remember the orderlies rushing in.

EDWARD. No more blood from him. No more urine, either.

MARTIN. They pulled the sheet up over his face.

EDWARD. Visible sighs of relief all round. No such diversion today.

Pause.

What have you there?

MARTIN. Shhhhhh! A Danish pastry.

EDWARD. But it is forbidden!

MARTIN. I have two. Would you care for one yourself?

EDWARD. It is forbidden. All those carbohydrates! (*Pause: whisper.*)
Please. Yes.

MARTIN. Hide it beneath your newspaper. Just break off a bit at a time.
That's what I always do. They have already taken my blood. So it
won't show up there. I have given them my urine. It won't show
there, either.

EDWARD. Look out! Nurse!

NURSE. Mr Johnson, please.

ALL. Who?

NURSE. Mr Johnson.

ALL. We don't know a Mr Johnson!

NURSE. Would you please all listen for your names to be called out.
Please!

EDWARD. Someone did leave the room. An old man. With a stick.

NURSE. I don't know if he's an old man with a stick or not! Please!
The sooner you can all see Doctor the sooner you can go.

MARTIN. Someone else left the room. A skeleton.

NURSE. A skeleton?

MARTIN. A survivor of sorts.

NURSE. A survivor? What do you mean?

WOMAN. Has Mrs Jenkins been called yet?

NURSE. As soon as Doctor gets to your file, you'll be called. Please pay
attention. Please! Just listen out for your names. That's all you have
to do. Please!

She goes.

EDWARD. Very touchy today.

MARTIN. Not the best of days.

EDWARD. Are you on the insulin?

MARTIN. The diet. And the tablets.

EDWARD. Then should you be eating the pastry?

MARTIN. Are you enjoying yours?

EDWARD. It's lovely!

MARTIN. How can they possibly find out? They have taken your blood.
You have given them your urine. I sometimes treat myself to a bar
of chocolate.

EDWARD. Sinful!

MARTIN. A marvellous thrill! I usually treat myself to one on a Thursday. Sometimes a Tuesday. Once, on a Wednesday. The sweetshop is a short walk from my home. By pacing my steps I can usually have consumed it by the time I reach my front door. Then the wrapper in the dustbin. And no one to know about it but me.

EDWARD. Have you seen this nurse before?

MARTIN. Not that I recall. But they all look the same to me now.

EDWARD. Not bearing up too well, by the look of it. Not completely in command of the situation. The stress of it all. She'll be ending up in psychiatric, if she's not too careful.

MARTIN. I had a spell in there once. Something went wrong with the noddle.

EDWARD. I had a week or two of it. It was like a holiday camp. All it lacked was a bar.

MARTIN. I had the odd bottle smuggled in. Perfect freedom.

EDWARD. Except for the drink.

MARTIN. And where is one, without a glass or two.

Pause.

If it is not the mind that ails you, then perhaps it is the body, but is it the mind that controls the body, or is it the body that controls the mind? Or so I once read. I read a lot after I had been to psychiatric. A lot of it seemed nonsense, of course. A lot of it completely far fetched. A lot of it going completely over my head. When it comes to medicine no one's too clear about anything at all, it seems to me.

EDWARD. Where are you going?

MARTIN. Just to have a look.

Pause.

And still they come. There are even more in the corridor than there was before.

EDWARD. Except for the torment inside my head, it was like a holiday in psychiatric. Stuffing you full of drugs to slow you down. Looking at you in the puzzled way they look at you and you looking back at them in the puzzled way you look at them. No one too sure about anything at all. Everyone much in the dark. Some things you tell them. A lot you withhold. Too near the knuckle, some of the things they ask. An intrusion.

VOICE (*on the tannoy we catch the name of Mrs Jenkins*). Would Mrs Jenkins please report to consulting room number four.

WOMAN. It's me.

MARTIN. You, madam.

WOMAN. They called out my name.

EDWARD. But you arrived here after me, madam. By rights I should be going before you.

WOMAN. But where do I go?

EDWARD. I don't know.

WOMAN. But didn't you hear?

EDWARD. I wasn't listening.

WOMAN. You heard my name being called.

MARTIN. I heard a name being called. But it wasn't my name that was being called. Of that I'm sure.

WOMAN. It was Jenkins. Mrs Jenkins. I'm sure of it. But which room?

EDWARD. I don't know which room, madam.

MARTIN. Sit down, madam. Nurse will come and fetch you.

WOMAN. But I have to go. They have called my name.

EDWARD. But where will you go?

WOMAN. I don't know. But I have to go. I have been called.

EDWARD. Nurse will come and fetch you.

WOMAN (*going*). I'm going. I have to go.

MARTIN. Will she ever be seen again, do you think? Another lost patient.

EDWARD. I sometimes feel I could lose myself in here. Never to be found again.

MARTIN. They would send a search party for you.

EDWARD. It is enormous. The building.

MARTIN. But we shall have a little peace now she has gone. Everyone else seems very subdued. Time to review one's life. For what it's worth. Time to go over the past.

Pause.

EDWARD. They say I am an interesting case. Interesting to them, that is. Of absolutely no interest to myself at all, apart from my appetites and certain thoughts that flicker through my mind. But as a case history, the interest is nil. Not being a medical man, do you see. Not having the slightest interest in my innards or what goes on thereabouts. But if I had a detachment about things, if I were the doctor and there was someone else masquerading as myself, then as the doctor I would have this detachment. I would be able to interest myself in the innards of others, as well as my own innards . . .

MARTIN. They never stop feeling themselves, you know.

EDWARD. Who?

MARTIN. Doctors. Always feeling their pulse. Pressing their stomachs. Pressing their sides. Listening to themselves with their stethoscopes.

EDWARD. How do you know?

MARTIN. A nurse once told me. It is the same with the nurses. They are always feeling themselves. Feeling for a lump here. A lump there. Half of them with a drink problem larger than one's own.

EDWARD. The nurses?

MARTIN. The doctors.

EDWARD. How do you know?

MARTIN. A nurse once told me.

EDWARD. Really?

MARTIN. In a shocking state some of them. Can't keep away from the ether, either.

EDWARD. Really?

MARTIN. Can't keep their hands out of the drugs cabinet.

EDWARD. Really?

MARTIN. Laying down the law to all and sundry.

EDWARD. Morbid!

MARTIN. What is?

EDWARD. To be enjoying one's glass of port and to be worrying about one's innards at the same time. To be continually worrying about the carbohydrates in a plate of crumpets. All the joy in life would go. If I were a doctor then perhaps I would enjoy the blackness of the humour as they seem to do. The levity of it all. But to be told to be moderate in all things, as I am told to be, then I wouldn't enjoy that at all. Not if I were a doctor. Not if I were having to tell myself. Not if I were my own physician.

MARTIN. Did you enjoy the pastry?

EDWARD. I haven't enjoyed anything quite so much in months. You don't, by chance, have another to spare?

MARTIN. I only brought the two with me. I usually have the two. I usually eat them both. If I were my own physician then I would give myself a blank cheque to carry on as I please. Enjoy what little life there is left to you: that would be my advice to myself. I have gout as well.

EDWARD. Really?

MARTIN. So they say. They've said a number of other things as well.

That I have done my liver a certain amount of damage. Each time I see a different doctor and each doctor puts a different stress on things. 'A slightly scarred liver,' says one. 'Your liver's taken a bit of a bashing,' says another. Which one do you believe? Which one of the comments is the more serious. The nearest the truth. When I leave the hospital I am always completely confused. Everything that is said to me seems to go completely over my head.

EDWARD. 'Keep away from the hospital if you possibly can,' was my father's advice to me. 'And keep away from the doctors too. They are more interested in your vices than a possible cure for you.' 'The smoking is not doing your lungs the least bit good,' they say. 'Give up the drink. Pack it in. The drink is not doing your liver the least bit good,' they tell me. But I have lived with my vices for years. They are like old friends to me. My pack of cigarettes is like an old friend. My mug of beer is also an old friend. I live in order to smoke. I live in order to sit on top of a bus and smoke my cigarette. It helps me to pass from one minute to the next. I exist in order to sup my beer. Better to sit there quietly drinking and smoking than to take the slightest scrap of notice of what is going on around you. Better to do that instead of depressing yourself by taking an interest in current affairs. Better to be doing that than to be poking about in the affairs of the people around you. Better that than to be sitting there with sullen thoughts going through your mind.

MARTIN. It is usually a stranger I see. The doctor. Someone you haven't seen before. They hardly look at you now. They have your file on the desk in front of them. And they read everything from the computer printout they have of you. The composition of your blood. The state of your liver.

EDWARD. I haven't enjoyed going to the doctor in years. Not since they took the ash trays out of the surgery waiting-rooms. A lot of the gaiety seemed to go out of life when they took the ash trays from the surgery waiting-rooms.

MARTIN. 'Do not smoke', it says. And there you are. Gasping for a smoke. A long wait. Nothing to do but twiddle your thumbs. Besides. It is my liver they are discussing. I am free to do as I choose with my liver. It's my liver. To have to give up all one's vices would be unbearable. Purgatory. Besides. When it comes to the drinking stakes I am a novice. There is an old man who walks past my house at six each evening. Half blind. Yet not a sober breath in fifty years. As long as you can see well enough to see the glass in front of you and raise it to your lips. That is all that matters. That is his view of life. 'I have simplified my life,' says he. 'I am now down to what is basic in life.'

Pause.

I trudge through the cemetery to get to the hospital.

EDWARD. But my friend, why take such a mournful walk?

MARTIN. It is a short cut for me. It is the easy way. And half way through the cemetery the hospital looms up at you. It casts its shadow across the graves. Even when it is a sunny day the shadow leaves a chill.

The NURSE *enters.*

NURSE. Mrs Jenkins, please.

EDWARD. Mrs Jenkins left the room several minutes ago, Nurse.

MARTIN. Her name was called.

NURSE. She's supposed to be with doctor, but she hasn't arrived at his room.

EDWARD. She received the summons from the Almighty and then she went.

NURSE. The Almighty?!

EDWARD. I sit here awaiting the summons myself.

NURSE. The summons?!

EDWARD. I was here long before Mrs Jenkins arrived, yet she has been seen before me.

NURSE. I'm sorry. But that sort of attitude won't get you anywhere.

MARTIN. I don't suppose he meant it.

EDWARD. Sorry, Nurse.

NURSE (*going*). Oh, dear. I do hope we haven't lost Mrs Jenkins. Please do listen for your names to be called out.

EDWARD. Touchy!

MARTIN. Psychiatric for her. Any day.

EDWARD. They stuff you full of drugs and let you sit there and rot.

MARTIN. I know. I've experienced it myself. Not quite right in the noddle. Not normal. A perfect nuisance, really.

EDWARD. They take your blood. And if your blood is compatible with the compatibility of the computer, they let you go. But no one really the wiser. Not having discovered, in the least, what it is that really ails you.

MARTIN. Still not quite right in the noddle. But if the computer tells them so, then you are released. Back into the outside world. But just as confused as you were when you left in the first place. One's demons still haunting one.

EDWARD. Give me good old-fashioned medicine any time. Instead of all the lights flashing on in front of you. I prefer the old-fashioned remedies.

Pause.

EDWARD. Sometimes the light is extinguished in people.

MARTIN. Sometimes.

EDWARD. A friend of mine. His liver in a shocking state. A politician. In a minor way. He had all the qualifications. A first class liar in every respect. He would trudge over the heath for hours thinking of his future. What he would do if he achieved real power. Then, one day, all the stuffing was knocked out of him. So he said.

MARTIN. Something unpleasant he heard?

EDWARD. No. He said it was a beautiful sunny day. He was walking down the road, his head full of wild dreams as usual, then, as he turned a corner, he felt all the stuffing being knocked out of him. It was like a balloon being deflated. He drinks heavily now, of course. Being reckless with his liver. His death wish obvious in the stoop of his shoulder.

MARTIN. It is the passing of the years.

EDWARD. He was in psychiatric for a while. Till they discharged him. Unable to do anything for him. Not the faintest idea of what really ailed him.

VOICE (*on the tannoy*). Would Mr Gerety please report to consulting room number one.

MARTIN. Would that be for you?

EDWARD. I pay no heed to it. Nurse will come and fetch me.

Pause.

I have lived in this district for most of my life. Except for the war years. For years I would pass the hospital by without even seeing it. Now it is sometimes in my dreams.

Pause.

MARTIN. I don't mind them taking the blood. It is the business with the piss pot that distresses me most. I am sometimes locked in that lavatory for an hour. Willing the bladder to work. Sometimes there is a bang on the door. A banging that might go on for minutes on end. Then, when you at last managed to achieve the sample required of you, you open the door and you find a queue of six or seven people. All with their piss pots in their hands. Some of the faces you know. Quite well. From the pub. But never recognition.

EDWARD. It once took me two hours to achieve the sample. When I had done, of course, everyone had gone home. I carried that piss pot around with me for a month. I gave it to them when I arrived for my next appointment. A month later when I returned again the physician was bright pink with amazement. He called his students in to look at me. 'He is a corpse,' he tells them. 'His urine has all the characteristics of someone who has been dead for a month.' He made a few other jokes like that, too.

MARTIN. It often seems to me that they are having a joke at my expense. I lie there on the bed feeling like death and all around the students are smiling at the banter of the physician. I try, sometimes to join in the laughter, not having the faintest idea of what the physician is saying and how it relates to my own well being. Sometimes they say to you, 'You needn't take off your underpants.' And you thank God for small mercies. At least he is not going to start cracking jokes at the expense of that part of one's anatomy. Then he starts to ask them questions. He chides them. He teases them. And all the while you lie there thinking you have been forgotten.

EDWARD. 'He's been dead for a month,' he said. That raised the biggest laugh of all. And he raised the printout for them all to see and the tears of merriment streamed down their faces. Then they went. Then someone came back and said I could go. And that would I come back in a month. And all the while wiping the tears from his eyes. Trying to hold back the laughter. 'What is wrong with me?' I ask. 'Yours is a very interesting case,' they say. 'Come back and see us in a month.'

Pause.

MARTIN. Whenever I come to the hospital now it seems to be full of the people I see in the pubs. When we meet in the pub we pass the time of day. But when we see each other in the hospital our eyes never meet. It is the same in the pub. We never mention to each other that we have seen each other in the hospital. It is not, it seems, the form. It is not the proper thing to do.

EDWARD. I sometimes see them in the pub. The people I've seen in the hospital. Trudging along the corridors with their slips of paper in their hands. Going for the X-ray. Going for the blood test. Each carrying their little piss pots. Looking very worried. Looking very glum. Yet when you see them later. In the pub. Not exactly smiling. But with quite a different demeanour from the demeanour they have shown in the hospital.

The NURSE *enters.*

NURSE. Mr Gerety?

EDWARD. Yes.

NURSE. Please!

EDWARD. Yes?

NURSE. Didn't you hear your name being called?

EDWARD. I heard nothing, Nurse.

NURSE. Doctor wants you. You are to go to consulting room number one.

EDWARD. You'll have to show me the way. I will get lost on my own.

NURSE. Very well. But quickly. We are running out of time.

Fade.

Mr Smith?

MARTIN. Yes?

NURSE. Have you seen the doctor?

MARTIN. I've just been to see him.

NURSE. Thank goodness. Something to be thankful for at last.

MARTIN. I didn't understand a word of what he said. It went straight over the top of my head as usual. I am to come back in a month. Nurse. Are you all right? You look distraught.

NURSE. It's been one of those days.

MARTIN. We all have days like that.

NURSE. I've lost four patients.

MARTIN. I am sorry.

NURSE. It's never happened before.

MARTIN. Dead?

NURSE. No. Lost. I've lost Mrs Jenkins, Mr Johnson, Mr Harris and Mr Brown. They are supposed to come into the system at one end and go out of it the other. It works quite well usually. Or should do. If everyone were to co-operate. They are lost. We have lost them. We can't send their files back to registry.

MARTIN. Are you new to this clinic?

NURSE. Yes. I was in psychiatric before I came down here. We used to lose people there, too, but it didn't seem to matter in psychiatric. You were expected to lose people in psychiatric. Sometimes we were glad to lose them. The difficult ones. But they don't like you losing people down here. Oh, dear!

MARTIN. You won't really have lost them. They'll still be in the building. Perhaps they'll turn up tomorrow.

NURSE. But there isn't another clinic for a month.

MARTIN. Mrs Jenkins won't have left the building. She only does what she's told to do. She probably turned a wrong corner. Lost somewhere in this great building.

NURSE. At least *you've* seen Doctor. Something to be thankful for.

MARTIN. Thankful for small mercies, Nurse. Always. Always be thankful for small mercies.

Fade.

Pub sounds.

EDWARD. My friend. There you are. I wondered if I'd see you.

MARTIN. Ah!

EDWARD. Unusual to see you here.

MARTIN. I decided not to take the short cut today. I have had enough of the cemetery. It is so cold there. I need warming.

EDWARD. Let me get you a drink. Here. Let me take your coat. It is warm in here. What can I get you to drink?

MARTIN. A pint of bitter.

EDWARD. Is it forbidden?

MARTIN. Yes.

EDWARD. I am on to my second pint. Both of them forbidden. And a small whisky. That is forbidden too.

He goes to the bar.

A pint of bitter please. (*To* MARTIN.) Would you like a whisky chaser with it?

MARTIN. I might have one later. I might stay here for a while.

EDWARD. I might stay for a while, too, my friend.

Pause.

There. Your pint.

MARTIN. Thank you.

EDWARD. The doctor is in the other bar. Drinking brandy. Large ones by the look of it.

MARTIN. Oh?!

EDWARD. The nurse is with him. She is disconsolate. He has a hand on her knee.

MARTIN. She is new to the clinic. She has come from psychiatric. As a nurse.

EDWARD. She'll be back there soon as a patient.

MARTIN. She has lost Mrs Jenkins.

EDWARD. I knew she would be lost. She didn't know where she was going. She will be wandering around those corridors for a month. Nothing to eat in all that time.

MARTIN. There is the cafeteria.

EDWARD. But, my friend, we have escaped. Back into the outside world again. Freedom yet again. At least we have achieved another day.

MARTIN. Yes. Another day.

EDWARD. And we will see tomorrow.

MARTIN. Yes. But not all the tomorrows.

EDWARD. No. Not all the tomorrows. But we shall see tomorrow. I am convinced of that. When is your next appointment?

MARTIN. A month from today.

EDWARD. What time?

MARTIN. Three-thirty.

EDWARD. My appointment is for three-thirty-five. So we shall see each other again.

MARTIN. Yes. We shall see each other again.

EDWARD. My friend, I am so glad I have got to know you. Why? I even look forward to my next appointment. Thinking that you will also be there will give me something to look foward to. I shall bring the Danish pastries next time.

MARTIN. Be sure to bring four. I like to have two.

EDWARD. And now we have escaped. For a month. A month in which to act and do as we please.

Some music from the juke box.

Friendship is so important. It is so rare a thing. And we are over this ordeal. For a month.

MARTIN. Yes we are.

EDWARD. Cheers, my friend.

MARTIN. Your good health!

They suddenly realise the significance of that last remark and they both start to chuckle.

EDWARD. And your good health, too, of course. Cheers, my friend!

MARTIN. Cheers!

EDWARD. Cheers!

KING CANUTE

by Barry Collins

For Andrew, Nan and Daniel

Barry Collins was born in Halifax in 1941. In 1970 he abandoned a
career in journalism to become a full-time writer. His first stage play,
And Was Jerusalem Builded Here?, was staged in 1972 at the Leeds
Playhouse, which later presented his children's play, *Beauty and the
Beast*. Other plays include *Judgement* (staged by the National Theatre
at the ICA in 1975, at the Royal Court Theatre in 1976, and at the
National Theatre itself in 1977); *The Strongest Man in the World*
(Nottingham Playhouse, 1978; Roundhouse, 1980); and *The Ice
Chimney* (Lyric Theatre, Hammersmith, 1980, following a preview at
the 1980 Edinburgh Festival where it won a 'Fringe First' award). For
television he has written *The Lonely Man's Lover* (BBC 'Play for Today',
1974); *The Witches of Pendle* (BBC, 1976); *The Hills of Heaven* (BBC,
1978, an adaptation for children); *Dirty Washing* (ITV 'Crown Court',
1984); and *Nada* (BBC 'Global Report' about Bogota, 1985).

King Canute was first broadcast on BBC Radio 3 on 10 March 1985. The cast was as follows:

HAROLD SMITH	Bernard Hill
MAUREEN SMITH	Judith Barker
LANDLADY	Rosalie Williams
SISTER	
SAMARITAN	Sally Edwards
ANNOUNCER	
OFFICER	
PILOT	Peter Wheeler
ANNOUNCERS	
AIRMAN	
DOCTOR	Paul Webster
INSPECTOR	

Director: Alfred Bradley
Running time, as broadcast: 50 minutes, 17 seconds.

Sea sounds. Seagulls.
Trombone: playing the opening chords of Beethoven's Fifth Symphony.
Sea sounds, nearer.

MAUREEN. Tide's coming in.

More seagulls.

MAUREEN. I said — tide's coming in.

HAROLD. Not today it isn't.

Trombone: again: peremptory — 'Rule Britannia'.
Sea sounds.

MAUREEN. Still coming in.

HAROLD. Never did believe in me, did you?

Sea sounds, even nearer.

MAUREEN. Put it this way, love: if you'd told me you were
King Canute.

HAROLD. Do I look like King Canute?

MAUREEN. Well, you've always spent a long time on the throne.

HAROLD. King Canute's a flaming racehorse.

Trombone: Dead March from 'Saul'.

MAUREEN. How much did you lose?

HAROLD. Five thousand.

MAUREEN. All five thousand?

HAROLD. He came second.

MAUREEN. And you backed him to win.

HAROLD. I could hardly back him each way.

MAUREEN. Why?

HAROLD. There were only two runners . . . The winner was Pharoah.

Seagulls.
Trombone: the first two lines of 'We Shall Overcome'.

HAROLD (*singing raucously*). We shall overcome some day . . .

MAUREEN. Daft beggar.

HAROLD. Moses did.

MAUREEN. What?

HAROLD. Overcome. Turn the tide. Beat Pharoah.

MAUREEN. It wasn't Moses. It was God. And let me tell you something, sunshine. God's the boss.

HAROLD. Aye, but is the boss God?

MAUREEN. You bet. Parting the Red Sea was just like combing his hair.

Trombone: plaintive 'Guide Me, O Thou Great Jehovah'.
Sea sounds, very near.

Know what time it is?

HAROLD. Half past six.

MAUREEN. In the morning.

HAROLD. Right.

MAUREEN. So what are you doing on the beach at Redcar at half past six in the morning?

HAROLD. I could ask you the same thing.

MAUREEN. I'm looking for my husband.

HAROLD. I'm changing the world.

MAUREEN. You're drunk.

HAROLD. Last night I was drunk. Last night I wanted to end it all. I sat down at the edge of the sea and fell asleep.

MAUREEN. What happened?

HAROLD. The tide went out.

MAUREEN. Typical.

HAROLD. When I woke up, there was nothing but sand. I was lonely. I started playing my trombone. And the tide turned. Far out. On the horizon. It came back to me. Like an answer.

MAUREEN. What was the question?

HAROLD. You've got no soul, that's your trouble.

MAUREEN. I've got no feeling. My feet are blue.

HAROLD. Put your shoes on.

MAUREEN. They'll stain.

HAROLD. Then get out of the bloody sea.

Sea sounds, all around.
Then the trombone: the first bars of 'The Times They Are
A'changin' '.

HAROLD (*singing*). ' — admit that the waters around you have
grown' . . .

More sea sounds. Seagulls.

MAUREEN (*farther away*). Harold, can I ask you something? I mean,
before you go under . . . Why did you bring your trombone all the
way from Bradford?

HAROLD. It's not my trombone. It's the firm's trombone. They want
it back.

MAUREEN. 'Cos you don't work there anymore?

HAROLD. They've disbanded the band. It belongs to the Official
Receiver.

Louder sea sounds.

MAUREEN (*still further away*). Look love, you might have lost your job,
but try and hang on to your marbles.

Rising sea sounds.
Trombone: 'Mad Dogs and Englishmen'.

MAUREEN (*shouting*). Harold. It's up to your chest.

Trombone declines into a gurgling noise, glug glug, glug . . .
The sound of waves breaking, seagulls crying.

The clatter of high heels in empty streets, and the slopping of wet shoes.

MAUREEN. I hope you're satisfied.

There is no reply.
The slopping stops.

'Cos you didn't just back the wrong horse, you blew your whole
redundancy pay.

The high-heeled shoes stop.

MAUREEN (*calling*). Harold.

HAROLD. Look at 'em. Curtains drawn. Fast asleep. I've been out at
six every day for twenty-five years. And where's it got me? (*Yelling:*)
Wake up.

MAUREEN. It's the seaside.

HAROLD (*yelling*). It's time you all woke up.

MAUREEN. Breakfast's not till eight.

Trombone: Reveille.
Silence.
Then the sound of a window being thrown up, and another, and another: a baby starts bawling, then another.

HAROLD (*yelling*). Do you know how many people are unemployed in Redcar?

More windows, more babies.

When are you going to do something about it?

The sound of bottles, buckets, plantpots etc, smashing to the ground.

VOICES (*in unison*). Bugger off.

Windows bang down, babies stop bawling.

MAUREEN. They're on holiday.

HAROLD. They don't care.

Trombone: opening bars of the 'Battle of Jericho', then HAROLD, belting out the words.

HAROLD (*singing*). 'Joshua fought the battle of Jericho and the walls came tumbling down.'

From a distance, coming nearer, the wail of a police siren.

MAUREEN. Oh lory.

The siren reaches a climax and stops. A car door slams. Windows up, bang, bang, bang; babies bawling.

OFFICER. Oi, Louis Armstrong.

HAROLD (*outraged*). Louis Armstrong?

MAUREEN. He's upset, officer. It's a family matter. We've suffered a terrible loss.

VOICES (*from above, separately*).
Is that why he's blowing the trombone? . . .
In a blue tuxedo? . . .
White flannels . . .
And a dickey-bow? . . .

OFFICER. All right, into the car.

Trombone: opening of the 'Marseillaise'.

OFFICER (*threatening*). Into the car.

The car doors open, then slam.
Windows bang down; babies stop bawling.

A doorbell rings.

MAUREEN. Trust me to forget the key.

> *The bell rings again.*
> HAROLD's *teeth are chattering.*

MAUREEN. Harold.

HAROLD. What?

MAUREEN. Your teeth are chattering.

> *The sound of locks being turned, bolts drawn, a door creaking open.*

LANDLADY. Yes?

MAUREEN. I'm Mrs Smith.

LANDLADY. Ah yes — Mrs Smith.

MAUREEN. The double room at the back.

LANDLADY. Ah yes — the back double.

MAUREEN. This is my husband.

LANDLADY. Are you sure it's not the late Mr Glenn Miller?

MAUREEN. It's my husband.

LANDLADY. I didn't notice a husband last night, Mrs Smith.

MAUREEN. I've only just found him.

LANDLADY. Really?

MAUREEN. On the beach.

LANDLADY. Ah yes — and would that be why he is steaming? Or would it be lust, Mrs Smith? Would it be hanky-panky? I said last night — when you asked for the back double — I said no hanky-panky.

> HAROLD *groans, teeth chattering.*

MAUREEN. Please, can we come in?

LANDLADY. Is your husband in the habit of wetting the doorstep?

MAUREEN. He'll catch his death of cold.

LANDLADY. My dear Mrs Smith, if Count Dracula can step ashore at Whitby, the late Mr Glenn Miller can walk out of the sea at Redcar. It's time something happened at Redcar. It's time something happened full stop.

> *The creak of the door opening.*

MAUREEN. Thank you.

> *The door closes, locks turn.*

It's a long story.

LANDLADY. I thought it might be.

The sound of feet on a staircase.

LANDLADY (*calling, from below*). Mrs Smith . . .

The footsteps stop.

One egg or two?

HAROLD (*shivering*). Where's the fire?

MAUREEN. It's central heating.

HAROLD. There used to be a fire.

MAUREEN. That was on our honeymoon.

Pause. More shivering.

Take your clothes off, then.

HAROLD. My hands have gone white.

MAUREEN. Here . . .

Sounds of undressing.

Best put 'em on the radiators . . . looks like a Chinese laundry . . .
(*Laughing.*) How d'you get seaweed down there?

Pause.

Want me to dry you?

HAROLD. If you like.

Towelling sounds.

MAUREEN. Know when my mother caught you in the bath? Watch
him, our lass, she said, he's a big lad is your Harold . . . Manage the
rest, can you?

More towelling.

HAROLD. Why did you suck up to that copper?

MAUREEN. So you wouldn't get arrested.

HAROLD. There's four million folk in the same boat as me.

MAUREEN. Only they haven't all sailed off to Redcar with the works'
trombone . . . Could have left a note.

HAROLD. Sorry.

MAUREEN. Aren't you always? . . . Get your little white bum into that
bed before I belt it.

Bedsprings — and again — and again . . . Silence.

MAUREEN. Harold — I'm waiting.

HAROLD. Shh.

MAUREEN. You don't usually keep me waiting.

HAROLD. Shh.

MAUREEN. Harold —

HAROLD. I'm trying to remember where I am.

MAUREEN. Is that supposed to be funny?

Bedsprings.

MAUREEN. Aaah . . .

HAROLD. I'm an Atlantic roller.

MAUREEN. What?

HAROLD. They take a long time — Atlantic rollers.

Bedsprings.

MAUREEN. Oooh . . . Couldn't we have a storm?

HAROLD. Gale force eight?

Bedsprings.

MAUREEN. Yes.

HAROLD. Iceland, Rockall, Mallin —

MAUREEN. Yes. Yes.

Bedsprings.

HAROLD. I'm passing the Outer Hebrides.

MAUREEN. S'lovely there.

HAROLD. Shh.

MAUREEN. In the Outer Hebrides.

Bedsprings.

HAROLD. I've been building up.

MAUREEN. I know.

HAROLD. All the way across.

Bedsprings.

MAUREEN. Mmmm . . .

HAROLD. There's only one place in the world —

Bedsprings.

MAUREEN. Mmmm.

HAROLD. Where you get these long rollers.

Bedsprings.

MAUREEN. Mmmm.

HAROLD. Each one comes two thousand miles.

Bedsprings.

MAUREEN. Mmmm . . . Where are we now?

HAROLD. North of South Uist.

Bedsprings, counter-pointed from here on with the words.

MAUREEN. Aaah.

HAROLD. Inishvickilaun.

MAUREEN. Yes.

HAROLD. Harris tweed.

MAUREEN. Yes.

HAROLD. Nearly there.

MAUREEN. Yes.

HAROLD. All that power.

MAUREEN. Yes.

HAROLD. Energy.

MAUREEN. Yes.

HAROLD. Crashing on the beach.

MAUREEN. Yes.

HAROLD. The white sand.

MAUREEN. Aaah.

HAROLD. East of Knocknamuir.

MAUREEN. Oh God.

Last creak. Silence.

Can we go back the other way?

HAROLD. There's only one way. Starting off Newfoundland — with a following wind . . . Imagine.

MAUREEN. What?

HAROLD. All the electricity we could generate — if only we could plug into the National Grid.

Trombone: light, soft blues phrases. Silence. . . .

HAROLD. Pass us a fag.

MAUREEN. They're wet.

Trombone: more blues, a little louder and sadder.

Is that how you feel?

HAROLD. How would *you* feel?

MAUREEN. How do you think I feel?

Trombone: long, sad notes.

HAROLD. Anyway, how did you find me?

MAUREEN. The window was open. I heard mating calls from the sea.

HAROLD. I could have been anywhere.

MAUREEN. Think I'm blind? You'd ringed the date on the calendar. And the horse in the paper . . . When I got back from work and you weren't there, I jumped straight on the train. Change at Leeds, York and Middlesborough . . .

HAROLD. Who's with the kids?

MAUREEN. They're not kids. Not any more . . . They can cope. For a few days. While we get something sorted — you and me.

More trombone: sadder than ever.

MAUREEN. We've to be out of here by ten.

HAROLD. Hell fire.

MAUREEN. I only booked one night.

HAROLD. I'm staying.

MAUREEN. What shall I tell the landlady?

HAROLD. You're having your second honeymoon.

MAUREEN. What are *you* having?

HAROLD. A nervous breakdown.

Suddenly, a great anguished blast on the trombone: 'The St James's Infirmary Blues'.

MAUREEN. Harold.

From above, and all around, sounds of knocking — on walls, floors, water pipes — and muffled shouts of protest.

No hanky-panky.

HAROLD. That's not hanky-panky.

Trombone: another burst of the blues. More knocking, louder protests.

MAUREEN. Stop it, Harold.

Now a knocking at the door, nearer, and the voice of the LANDLADY, *from outside.*

LANDLADY. Mrs Smith.

MAUREEN. Yes.

LANDLADY. Is your husband in pain?

HAROLD (*shouting*). Yes.

LANDLADY. Perhaps he's prefer breakfast in bed.

MAUREEN. If it's not too much trouble . . .

Soft, burbling sounds from the trombone.

Breakfast noises: plates rattling, eggs being cracked.

LANDLADY. Do you do 'Little Brown Jug'?

HAROLD (*mouth full*). No.

Pause.
More plates; tea pouring.

LANDLADY. 'Chatanooga Choo-Choo'?

HAROLD. No.

LANDLADY. Pity.

MAUREEN. It was a brass band.

LANDLADY. Ah.

MAUREEN. The Bradford and Bingley.

LANDLADY. Are you sure it wasn't a building society?

Trombone: 'Bless This House' — a full verse, played with feeling.

Oh Mr Smith — how beautiful . . . to be able to play so beautifully — it's a gift.

Silence.

MAUREEN. They were at the Albert Hall in 1973.

LANDLADY. And where are they now?

HAROLD. Exactly.

LANDLADY. Oh dear.

HAROLD. It's progress.

MAUREEN. It's those cheap Belgian carpets — sending our folk down the Swannee.

HAROLD. It's inevitable . . . isn't it.

LANDLADY (*puzzled*). What?

HAROLD. Unemployment. Like the tide — coming in, going out. What the blazes are you supposed to do?

LANDLADY. Oh, there's always something you can do.

Silence.
The sound of plates, etc.

LANDLADY. I once went to the theatre.

HAROLD. What good's going to the theatre?

LANDLADY. It was a play about war — some war or other — telling us it was a bad thing — the war — as if we didn't know . . . (*She stops.*)

MAUREEN. Yes?

LANDLADY. Right at the end, a lovely young actor held up a box with three drawers. He opened one drawer and out flew a butterfly — meaning peace, you see. And the same with the second drawer — another butterfly came fluttering over our heads . . . From the third drawer, he took the last butterfly by the wing-tips and set fire to it with a lighter . . . I was in the front stalls, on the aisle. Without even thinking, I climbed up on the stage and snatched the butterfly from him. It crumbled to ashes in my hand . . . I felt so silly. I turned to the audience. I said: 'I'm sorry — it was made of paper. I just wanted to show there's always something you can do' . . .

The LANDLADY's *voice fades to silence.*

Trombone: 'My Funny Valentine'.

MAUREEN. Harold — can't we talk about it? We used to talk about things — before you turned into a trombone.

HAROLD. Try singing.

MAUREEN. What shall I sing?

HAROLD (*singing*). 'My funny valentine . . .'

MAUREEN (*singing*). 'Sweet, comic valentine . . .'

BOTH (*singing*). 'You make me smile with my heart.'

Silence.

MAUREEN. It'll be all right . . . won't it?

HAROLD. Everything's changed.

MAUREEN. We still love each other . . . That's something to hang on to — isn't it? . . . no matter what happens.

HAROLD. Nobody knows what's going to happen.

MAUREEN. To us. I'm talking about us.

HAROLD. I'm talking about life.

MAUREEN. Couldn't we stick to Bradford?

HAROLD (*exasperated*). Look — suppose the sun stopped rising.

MAUREEN. We'd all be dead.

HAROLD. Not just in Bradford.

MAUREEN. It'd be Armageddon.

HAROLD. Have you had those Jehovah's Witnesses round again?

MAUREEN. Only for insurance. Same as I buy pegs from gypsies.

HAROLD groans.
A shoe, knocking on the floor, in Morse Code rhythm.

Now what are you doing?

HAROLD. Sending an SOS.

MAUREEN. Who to?

HAROLD. Whoever it may concern.

MAUREEN. It's half past three. Everybody's on the beach.

From above, a similar knocking, in reply.

HAROLD. Listen.

More knocking.

HAROLD (*translating*). On . . .

Knocking.

your . . .

Knocking.

bike.

The knocking stops.

That settles it.

MAUREEN. Settles what?

HAROLD. Which side he's on.

MAUREEN. Who?

HAROLD. God.

MAUREEN. God?

HAROLD. The feller upstairs.

On the trombone: a loud raspberry.

MAUREEN. Harold.

HAROLD. Look — suppose the sun came out tomorrow and we were all
dead anyway.

MAUREEN (*trying hard*). 'Cos of a war, you mean?

HAROLD. Too true. And where's your God then? Where's your crystal
ball? Where's your Pisces and your Capricorn? Where's Albert
Einstein? Where's Marx and Engels? Where's Pavlov's dog? Where's
your supply and demand if the whole giddy grocery's gone up in
smoke? (*Pause.*) See what I'm driving at?

MAUREEN. No.

HAROLD. Nothing's inevitable — not if there's no one left for it to
happen to.

MAUREEN. Not even the end of the world?

HAROLD. Not once you can blow yourselves to smithereens. It's people that make things like they are. Maybe other people can make them different.

A window being raised.

(*Shouting:*) Give us back our bloody world.

A window banging down.
Then a line of blaring music: 'Seventy-six Trombones'.
From all around, above and below, on the walls, down the pipes, loud knocking noises.

MAUREEN. Must be later than I thought. They're all home for tea.

HAROLD (*excited*). Well, I'll be damned.

MAUREEN. You said it.

HAROLD. Look at this map on the wall . . . 'King Canute's Rock'. About a mile out. From the next bay . . . 'Uncovered at low tide'.

MAUREEN (*wailing*). Harold.

Her voice fades away.

The sound of waves, crashing on rocks . . . from a distance, over the sea, the opening lines of 'Jerusalem', played on a trombone.

The sound of a telephone ringing, at the other end of the line.

VOICE. Hello, the Samaritans.

Pips, and coins being inserted, in a call-box.

MAUREEN (*breathless*). Hello . . .

VOICE. Can I help you?

MAUREEN. It's not me — it's my husband.

VOICE. I see.

MAUREEN. When I woke up, he'd gone . . . I only nodded off.

VOICE. How long ago?

MAUREEN. After the nine o'clock news . . . The unemployment figures always upset him.

VOICE. Perhaps he's drowning his sorrows.

MAUREEN. No — I think he's just drowning.

VOICE. Pardon?

MAUREEN. He's on King Canute's Rock.

VOICE. But the tide's coming in.

MAUREEN (*desperate*). I know.

VOICE. Haven't you called the police?

MAUREEN. They wouldn't listen.

VOICE. Why?

MAUREEN. They've nearly arrested him once already.

VOICE. What for?

MAUREEN. Playing the trombone on Acacia Avenue.

Her voice fades away.

More waves, breaking over rocks . . .
Above the sea sounds, nearer now, the trombone: 'Yellow Submarine'.

Telephone pips. Coins going into the phone box. The pips stop.

MAUREEN (*urgent*). Could *you* call the police? Call the coastguards. Call the lifeboat. Call anything.

VOICE. I can try.

MAUREEN. When's high tide?

VOICE. Midnight.

MAUREEN. Oh lory, it's quarter to twelve.

Fade out on MAUREEN's voice.

Nearer still, the trombone, over loud sea sounds, playing 'The Last Post'.

MAUREEN. I heard him — on the breeze — I heard him.

LANDLADY. I hear him every night.

MAUREEN. Who?

LANDLADY. The late Mr Glenn Miller. I always leave the window open. He steals in from the deep, where he drowned, bearing his slide trombone . . . (*She quivers.*) . . . like Lancelot coming to Guinevere.

MAUREEN. It's Harold.

LANDLADY. What is he playing?

MAUREEN. 'The Last Post'.

Fade out on MAUREEN's voice

Waves, close up, crashing over HAROLD and his rock.

HAROLD. Sorry, Maureen. Didn't mean it. Tide came round the back of me — in the dark — while I was baying at the moon.

A big wave; gurgling sounds.

HAROLD (*gasping for air*). Must've got it wrong about King Canute . . . (*He shudders.*) Can't even swim.

Another wave; more gurgling.

(*Bigger gasps.*) I'm hanging on by the limpets, Maureen . . . It's the soft, sticky bits you hang on with if you're a limpet . . . If the limpets let go, I'm a goner.

HAROLD *cries out.*
Another wave.
Choking noises.
Now his voice sounds hollow, echoing, with the waves in the background.

Maureen — I can see myself, spread on the rock, down there, like a daddy-long-legs on a sink. Suppose it's what *you'd* see if we had a mirror over the bed . . . Only he's not done yet, our Harold — he's hanging on for dear life, with his trombone slung over one arm, waiting for his luck to change . . . (*Calling:*) Stick tight, Harold.

Now HAROLD's *own voice again:*

(*Calling back:*) I am sticking tight, you daft beggar.

The sea, close up. Another wave. Choking sounds.

Help . . . Help . . . Help.

Suddenly, loud and very near, through the sea sounds and HAROLD's *cries, comes the noise of a helicopter, hovering, above, and a* MAN's *voice, over a hailer or loudspeaker.*

AIRMAN. Mr Smith.

HAROLD (*to himself*). Who's that?

AIRMAN. Mr Smith.

HAROLD. Blimey — a great light in the sky. And a great wind, parting the waters.

AIRMAN. Harold Smith.

HAROLD. And a voice out of the storm.

AIRMAN. We're dropping a ladder.

HAROLD. And a ladder — descending from above . . . It's Jacob's ladder.

AIRMAN. Can you hear me, Mr Smith?

HAROLD. I must be dead.

AIRMAN. Mr Smith.

HAROLD (*shouting*). Am I dead?

AIRMAN. Can you climb the ladder?

HAROLD. Not if I'm dead.

AIRMAN. Don't panic — we're coming lower.

Louder helicopter sounds and, through them, Strauss's 'Zarathustra' theme on a trombone.

AIRMAN (*alongside*). Mr Smith — you won't be needing your trombone.

HAROLD. In heaven, you mean.

AIRMAN. It's not heaven: it's a helicopter.

HAROLD. Well, I reckon that beats a ferry boat.

AIRMAN. Give me your hand.

HAROLD. You haven't any wings.

AIRMAN. I'm only the navigator.

HAROLD. Angels have wings.

AIRMAN. I'm the idiot who dangles off ladders six feet above the sea trying to save nutters in blue tuxedos and white flannels who think they're King Canute.

Another burst from 'Zarathustra'.

All right, keep your trombone.

HAROLD. It's not just a trombone.

AIRMAN. Stand still while I get this harness round you.

HAROLD. It's the Aeolian Harp.

AIRMAN (*grunting*). Arms up.

HAROLD. It's Orpheus's lyre. It's the pipes of Pan.

The crackle of a radio.

AIRMAN. Foxtrot two to foxtrot one.

HAROLD. It plays the music of the spheres.

PILOT. Foxtrot one, receiving.

AIRMAN. Customer secure. Winch him up.

HAROLD. Yes — take me to your leader.

The whine of the winch — and, still, the helicopter noise and the ocean.

AIRMAN. Come on Gabriel — blow your horn.

On the trombone: 'Fly Me to the Moon', receding up into the sky.

Aboard the helicopter: engine noise, from inside the cabin.
Trombone: still 'Fly Me to the Moon', but much closer.

PILOT (*bawling*). Cut it out.

More trombone.

There's no room.

A louder blast.

Ouch.

The trombone lurches.
The helicopter engine roars to a crescendo, then levels out again.

Lunatic.

HAROLD. I needed bottom F.

AIRMAN (*puffing and blowing*). Steady on skipper — nearly threw me off the ladder.

PILOT. This idiot belted me in the neck with his trombone.

HAROLD. Slide comes full out for bottom F.

Another blast.

PILOT. Ouch.

Again, briefly, the engine howls, then stabilises.

AIRMAN (*on the radio*). Foxtrot to base. Madman aboard.

HAROLD. Give it here.

Sounds of struggle.

HAROLD (*through the radio crackle*): Smith to God. Are you receiving me? Over.

PILOT. For pity's sake.

HAROLD. Smith to God. Come in God. Over.

PILOT. Shut him up.

AIRMAN. What with?

PILOT. Your imagination.

HAROLD. Smith to God. Smith to God —

The sound of a hard object striking bone . . . with reverberations.
Fade engine noise.

A mental hospital. MAUREEN *is consulting a* CONSULTANT.

MAUREEN. How is he, Doctor?

DOCTOR. Lucky to be alive.

MAUREEN. They shouldn't have hit him so hard . . . dented the trombone.

Pause.

DOCTOR. Mrs Smith, there's something I must tell you.

MAUREEN (*alarmed*). Oh lory.

DOCTOR. About King Canute.

MAUREEN. Don't say he won.

DOCTOR. In life, Mrs Smith, there's usually a middle way.

MAUREEN. What are you — some kind of Social Democrat?

DOCTOR. I'm a realist.

MAUREEN. Well, we're Labour.

DOCTOR. Is that why your husband was committing suicide?

MAUREEN. He wasn't committing suicide.

DOCTOR. Then what *was* he doing?

MAUREEN. Making his point . . . Can't a man make his point anymore?

DOCTOR. My dear Mrs Smith, if your husband had to be winched from a small rock, a mile out to sea, at high tide, in pitch darkness, isn't the taxpayer entitled to ask whether the point was worth making?

MAUREEN (*protesting*). He's lost his job.

DOCTOR. I fear he's lost touch with reality.

MAUREEN. It's not right.

DOCTOR. Reality, Mrs Smith, is hardly a matter of right and wrong: reality is what happens . . . as King Canute realised when he sat on his throne at the water's edge and shook his sceptre at the sea.

MAUREEN. Oh, that King Canute.

DOCTOR. Once the waves reached his waist, the royal servants lifted him out, and he spent the rest of his life being a very good king.

MAUREEN. Why?

DOCTOR. Because he had learned the limits of his power. Unlike your husband, who appears to have no idea of his own limits at all.

MAUREEN. You mean his place.

DOCTOR. I mean his limits. How many people, these days, believe they can change the world? And look how they end up — sedated, confined to bed, in a straitjacket.

MAUREEN. I warned you not to take away his trombone. He's probably got withdrawal symptoms.

DOCTOR. Mrs Smith, your husband's trombone almost lost a Royal Navy helicopter . . . Notwithstanding the fact that he seems to think he's dead.

MAUREEN. Let me see him.

DOCTOR. Out of the question.

MAUREEN. Why?

DOCTOR. If he thought you were dead, too, anything could happen.

MAUREEN. I'm not dead.

DOCTOR. Ah, but could you convince him? He insists I'm St Peter, come to hear his sins.

MAUREEN. Sins? Harold? The only sin Harold ever managed was with a blonde on a pile of Sultanas.

DOCTOR. Sultanas?

MAUREEN. Sultana carpets.

DOCTOR. Forgive me — he swears he did it over and over again.

MAUREEN. Yes, all on the same afternoon.

DOCTOR. My dear Mrs Smith, every man must have more than one afternoon on his conscience.

MAUREEN. Not my Harold. Harold's a good man. You can't keep him here, all tied up and fast asleep.

DOCTOR. Indeed I can.

MAUREEN. He's just upset.

DOCTOR. I can restrain him until he shows signs of adjusting to the real world.

MAUREEN. We'll see about that.

A chair scraping on the floor.

DOCTOR. The best we can hope for, Mrs Smith, is to ameliorate the inevitable.

MAUREEN. I said we'll see about that.

The loud banging of a door.

The ethereal sound of the trombone, playing 'I am Sailing'. It is heard throughout the scene, behind HAROLD's *slightly echoing, 'unconscious' voice.*

HAROLD. I can fly, you know. I've got wings. Well, not wings, exactly. More of a sail. Or a shroud. No, a sail — a golden sail. And I'm lying in it, like a hammock, all rolled up, so I can't move. It won't look like a sail, not from down there. Does it look like a shroud? Maybe a cocoon. No, a sail — a golden sail. If I could move, just roll over, then it would unfurl, this sail. It must be a mile across. Imagine. I can feel it, fastened to my hands and my feet, waiting to billow out, waiting to unfurl me. If only I could breathe. If I could breathe, I could unfurl myself. Then you'd see this golden sail, billowing through the sky, beating as I breathed, as I stretched myself, like spars, a mile across my shoulders, as I flew, and flew. I could go anywhere. It's endless. I can see past the sun, past the first stars, out of the galaxy, through a million galaxies, all waiting for me. Why can't I move? There's no friction up here. Once you start, you just gather speed, don't you? Through all time, all space. On your great golden sail. Breathing in, breathing out. Let me breathe, damn you. I can't breathe. How can I start if I can't even breathe?

Fade out voice and trombone music.

The tinkle of tea cups.

MAUREEN. Got to get him out somehow.

LANDLADY. Shall I pour?

MAUREEN. They say he's in a dream world, talking gibberish.

LANDLADY. Nothing like a good cup of tea.

The sound of tea being poured.

MAUREEN. It's because he thinks so much.

LANDLADY. Milk?

More pouring.

MAUREEN. He's always thinking about things — real things.

LANDLADY. Sugar?

Stirring.

MAUREEN. Humus toilets.

LANDLADY. Really.

Tinkling cups

MAUREEN. We have one in the back garden.

LANDLADY. What?

MAUREEN. A humus toilet.

LANDLADY. Ah.

MAUREEN. And a solar panel in the roof. If they'd give us planning permission, he'd build his own windmill. Natural things, see. Harold's a homeopathist. If he was born again, he'd probably be a Chinese foot doctor . . . Harold thinks a lot about the Chinese.

LANDLADY. Let's face it, Mrs Smith, there are a lot of Chinese to think about. (*Pause.*) Is anything wrong?

MAUREEN. You're not listening.

LANDLADY. On the contrary. Something's staring me in the face. From the evening newspaper. On the settee.

The crinkle of newspaper.

Listen . . . (*Reading:*) 'Sir Lancelot's last charge.'

MAUREEN (*scornful*). Sir Lancelot?

LANDLADY. Read it yourself.

The crackle of newspaper.

MAUREEN (*reading*). 'Redcar's favourite racehorse . . . ' (*She stops.*)
Oh no, not on your nelly, not another flaming racehorse.

LANDLADY. Read the whole story.

MAUREEN. What am I supposed to bet with, anyway — peanuts?

LANDLADY. Leave that to me.

MAUREEN *starts the story again — her scorn slowly turning to
fascination.*

MAUREEN. 'Redcar's favourite racehorse, the no-hope gelding,
Sir Lancelot, owned by a syndicate of redundant steelmen, bids
farewell to his home fans tomorrow. Sir Lancelot, never yet a winner,
runs against the unbeaten Kondratieff over six furlongs in a two-horse
sprint. Will the 50-1 outsider's luck change at the last? The form-book
says it's impossible. The steelmen claim the impossible might just
happen . . .

The crackle of newspaper.

LANDLADY. Now what do you think?

Pause.

MAUREEN. Why not? Yes — why bloody not? What have I got to lose?

LANDLADY. Oh Mrs Smith, wouldn't it be wonderful if Sir Lancelot
could rescue a damsel in distress?

The great cheer of a racecourse crowd. Over the noise can be heard the
COURSE ANNOUNCER, *commentating, as if from the back of a
grandstand.*

ANNOUNCER. They're off . . . And Kondratieff streaks clear from the
start . . . The odds-on favourite is four lengths up at the furlong
post . . . Sir Lancelot — eight lengths adrift.

*Suddenly, the continuous crowd babble turns to a mass howl of
surprise.*

CROWD. Oooh.

ANNOUNCER. And Kondratieff's down. Kondratieff came a cropper on
the curve. His legs gave way beneath him.

Another crowd roar.

Sir Lancelot sweeps past. Sir Lancelot in the lead. Sir Lancelot is going to win.

Another roar.

Kondratieff's back on his feet. The favourite's giving chase — thirty lengths behind . . . Into the last furlong, it's Sir Lancelot, by twenty lengths.

The crowd roar is constant and building.

Ten lengths now — Sir Lancelot — with a hundred yards to go . . . Five lengths, and Kondratieff closing fast . . . Last twenty yards — Sir Lancelot by a length and a half . . . Sir Lancelot's holding on — Sir Lancelot — at the post, it's Sir Lancelot, by a short head — Sir Lancelot has won . . . Sir Lancelot has won.

The crowd roar reaches a crescendo — and cuts.

MAUREEN (*softly*). I've never seen so much money.

LANDLADY (*whispering*). Not all at once.

MAUREEN. In one pile.

Pause.

LANDLADY. Are we in church, Mrs Smith?

MAUREEN. No.

LANDLADY. Then why are we whispering?

MAUREEN. I'm not whispering. I'm hoarse — with shouting for Sir Lancelot.

LANDLADY. Sweet Sir Lancelot. Look what he won for us. Shekels, Mrs Smith, spondulics, bawbees, filthy lucre, loaves and fishes . . . (*Pause.*) Shall we proceed to business? . . . Item: five on-course bookmakers, each at twenty pounds. Item: four town bookmakers, at twenty-five pounds. Item: two hundred pounds on the totalisator. All bets placed at fifty to one, earning a total of twenty thousand pounds — minus your stake of four hundred and ten pounds, including tax, which I hereby reclaim. Now, five thousand pounds, I trust, will wipe out your husband's memory of King Canute. The remaining fifteen thousand pounds will purchase, from the Official Receiver, the uniforms and instruments of the Bradford and Bingley Brass Band, and thereafter provide for its expenses . . . Agreed?

MAUREEN. Agreed. (*Pause.*) How can I ever thank you?

LANDLADY. My dear Mrs Smith, simply play one concert each summer at the Floral Hall, Redcar, consisting of the music of the late Mr Glenn Miller.

MAUREEN (*sly*). And his slide trombone.

LANDLADY (*impassioned*). And his slide trombone.

The jaunty sound of the 'Floral Dance', with full brass band . . .
Eventually, through the music, comes the angry voice of a WARD
SISTER — *and, close behind, the mental hospital* CONSULTANT.

SISTER. Who's playing havoc on my ward?

The music dribbles away.

DOCTOR. What the dickens do you think you're doing?

MAUREEN. The 'Floral Dance'.

SISTER. This is a mental hospital.

MAUREEN. We're visiting.

SISTER. I allow two visitors per bed, not an entire brass band.

MAUREEN. We're visiting everybody.

DOCTOR. No, Mrs Smith — you're trespassing.

MAUREEN. My husband's friends have come to cheer him up — all the
way from Bradford.

SISTER. I don't care if they've come from Timbuctoo.

MAUREEN. If we do some of Harold's favourite tunes, it might bring
him back to his senses.

DOCTOR. Too late.

MAUREEN. Why?

DOCTOR. He's lost them altogether. Only a madman would judge all
human life by a single Latin phrase — 'cui bono' . . . 'who gets the
gravy?'

MAUREEN. What's mad about that?

DOCTOR. Before anyone gets the gravy, Mrs Smith, someone else has
to manufacture it.

MAUREEN. Oh, anyone can cook the gravy. Why does it never get right
round the table?

DOCTOR. You're as mad as he is.

MAUREEN. Fine. Let me take him home and we can be mad together.

DOCTOR. Impossible. I've just committed him.

SISTER. He's due for electric shock treatment.

MAUREEN. Hear that, lads? We're in the nick of time.

*The sound of rushing footsteps, the sides of the bed being let
down, etc.*

DOCTOR. This is illegal.

SISTER. It's kidnapping.

MAUREEN. How can I kidnap my own husband?

DOCTOR. Under Section 28 of the Mental Health Act, 1961, he belongs to us.

HAROLD is heard groaning, amidst sounds of frenzied activity.

HAROLD. Can't breathe.

MAUREEN. Get the straitjacket off him.

DOCTOR. Call the police.

SISTER. Someone call the police.

MAUREEN. Trombone's behind the cupboard.

DOCTOR (*yelling*). You'll all go to gaol — to gaol, do you understand?

The sound of marching feet, and the band, playing 'Men of Harlech', all receding into the distance.

An ANNOUNCER's *voice, as in a radio news bulletin.*

ANNOUNCER. Here is the news. North Yorkshire police are hunting the twenty-four members of a brass band who today stole their lead trombonist from a Redcar mental hospital.

The click of a radio being switched off.
Silence.

HAROLD. They'll find us.

MAUREEN. Let them.

HAROLD. Can't go to ground with the whole Bradford and Bingley.

MAUREEN. Not for long. (*She laughs.*)

Silence.

Feeling better now?

HAROLD. I feel like Paul on the road to Damascus . . . I'll never be the same again.

Bedsprings.

MAUREEN. Feels just the same to me.

HAROLD. Mmmm.

Bedsprings.

MAUREEN. Can I be an Atlantic roller?

HAROLD. You're the Pacific.

MAUREEN. Am I?

Bedsprings.

HAROLD. Mmmm — I could drown in the Pacific.

MAUREEN. Not yet, Harold . . . not yet.

Bedsprings.

Where are we?

HAROLD. You tell me.

Bedsprings.

MAUREEN. Passing Easter Island.

HAROLD. Where the statues stand.

MAUREEN. And the giant turtles dance.

Bedsprings.

HAROLD. Mmmm.

MAUREEN. And the whales dive.

Bedsprings.

HAROLD. And the dolphins leap.

Bedsprings — counterpointed now.

MAUREEN. Oh yes, oh yes, I'm coming ashore.

HAROLD. On the coasts of Mandalay.

MAUREEN. Where the flying fishes play.

HAROLD. Mmmm.

MAUREEN. I can smell the jacaranda trees.

HAROLD. And the magnolia.

MAUREEN. And the passion flowers.

HAROLD. Mmmm.

MAUREEN. Aah . . .

Bedsprings cease.
Silence.

HAROLD. Where did you learn about the Pacific?

MAUREEN. You'd be surprised.

Suddenly, like a war-whoop, the trombone, playing the opening bars of 'Ilkley Moor', the Yorkshire anthem. From all around, above and below, come answering calls, on cornet, tuba etc. a line at a time, ending, in unison, on 'Ilkley Moor b'aht 'at' . . .
Silence.
Then the wail of police sirens, coming nearer.

Oh lory.

Sirens approach and stop. A POLICE INSPECTOR's voice is heard, over a megaphone, from outside.

INSPECTOR. All right, Mr Smith, we know you're in there. (*Silence.*) Are you coming quietly?

From the whole band, a big raspberry.

Or do we have to smash the door down to get you?

The sound of a window being thrown up.

HAROLD (*calling*). What, all of us? We've built a barricade. There's food for a month.

The window slams down. A door creaks open.

LANDLADY. Isn't it exciting? The siege of Acacia Avenue. I always thought something would happen in Redcar.

Again the INSPECTOR*'s voice is heard, over the megaphone, from outside.*

INSPECTOR. Mr Smith — we're prepared to negotiate.

The window goes up.

HAROLD. While you fetch the SAS.

INSPECTOR. Not for small fry.

HAROLD. What about a compromise? Get me on that radio show, where folk phone in and vote . . . Give me five minutes and I'll accept the majority verdict.

The window bangs down.

MAUREEN. Harold, are you sure?

HAROLD. Well, we can't stay here for ever.

The brass band: 'Cornet Carillon'. Then the ANNOUNCER.

ANNOUNCER (*on the radio*). Welcome to 'Voice of the People'. Tonight, Mr Harold Smith, the runaway trombonist, besieged in a seaside boarding house, will ask *you*, the people, to decide whether or not he is insane . . . Are you there, Mr Smith?

HAROLD (*close up, as on a telephone*). I'm here.

ANNOUNCER. The floor is yours.

HAROLD. Er, hello everybody. I just want to say this . . . when I got the sack, I didn't feel like a real person any more — they even took my trombone . . . Another thing. Some smart arses tell you unemployment makes the wheels go round. That's baloney. With computers, we can make enough wealth for us all, if it's shared out right — and the work's shared out, too. Snag is: who decides — and who gets the gravy? I mean, we don't want high priests in white coats poisoning us all with nuclear power stations . . . And another thing: my kids — what's their future? Brought 'em up wrong, see. Taught 'em to work hard and study, then God or the Queen or the Labour Party or some other grand panjandrum would give 'em a better life. As if they could leave it to somebody else. And you can't, can you?

You've got to get involved. Unless we want big brother and the white coats turning us into slaves who'll lie down and die quietly on social security while they slurp up all the flaming gravy.

The telephone receiver slamming down.

ANNOUNCER (*on the radio*). Thank you, Mr Smith . . . And next, our psychiatric report — from the consultant in charge of the case.

DOCTOR (*on the radio*). Subject: Harold Smith, aged 42, redundant carpet weaver. Diagnosis: complete emotional and spiritual collapse. Symptoms: gambling, assault, attempted suicide, abandonment of family and musical terrorism, of a peculiarly virulent form, which has already infected two dozen jobless instrumentalists and could become epidemic among the unemployed. In sum: Mr Smith clings, limpet-like, to outmoded styles of labour, coupling communitarian delusions with resistance both to authority and the gospel message (Matthew 26, verse 11): 'For ye have the poor always with you', by which the Lord Jesus, divine harbinger of the market economy, clearly meant that poverty is essential to a balanced society.

Loud studio applause.

ANNOUNCER (*on the radio*). Thank you, doctor . . . Over now to our panel of listeners, selected for age, area and aptitude to produce a cross-section of the voting population . . . Panellists: will you please use our instant computer link-up to answer the following question: is Harold Smith mad — or is he sane?

Brief blip-blip-blip sounds.

And here's the result. Mad — forty-four per cent. Sane — twenty-nine per cent. Don't know, don't care, can't tell the difference — twenty-seven per cent. . . . Sorry, Mr Smith, but that is the 'Voice of the People'.

Louder studio applause.

The radio clicking off.

MAUREEN (*upset*). Now what do we do?

HAROLD. Ask for a second opinion.

MAUREEN. Harold — they're going to cut out your frontal lobes and put them in a pickle jar.

HAROLD. They haven't a mandate.

MAUREEN (*incredulous*). Mandate?

HAROLD. Less than half the voters said I was mad.

MAUREEN. We're talking about the nuthouse, not the House of Commons.

HAROLD. I only need a fifteen per cent swing.

MAUREEN. Harold, do you want me to be married to a zombie?

HAROLD. With proportional representation —

MAUREEN. You don't support proportional representation.

HAROLD. Well, if I did, I'd have been sane.

MAUREEN (*thoughtfully*). I suppose you could always repent.

HAROLD. You mean 'recant'.

MAUREEN. Like in the Inquisition.

HAROLD. They wouldn't believe me.

MAUREEN. Try, Harold. Go back on the radio. Admit you were wrong.

HAROLD. I wasn't wrong.

MAUREEN. Does it matter?

HAROLD. Course it matters.

MAUREEN. Not without your frontal lobes, love. Without your frontal lobes, you won't know the difference. Not to mention the visiting. It'll cost a fortune, the visiting. On the train. And the kids. With a lunatic for a father. How will that sound at job interviews?

Pause.

HAROLD. Do *you* think I'm mad?

MAUREEN. I think you're the loveliest man I ever met . . . That's why I don't want to lose you.

A police siren, coming nearer.

Oh lory.

And nearer.

Repent, Harold.

And nearer.

Confess.

And nearer.

Harold — please.

The siren stops.
The sound of the window being thrown up, then the voice of the
POLICE INSPECTOR, *over a megaphone.*

INSPECTOR. Don't do it, Mr Smith.

HAROLD. What?

INSPECTOR. Throw yourself out of the window.

HAROLD. I've no intention of throwing myself out of the window.

INSPECTOR. Good.

HAROLD. Just get me back on the radio.

INSPECTOR. I've come to send you home.

HAROLD. Home?

INSPECTOR. To Bradford.

HAROLD (*suspicious*). What for?

INSPECTOR. Cuts.

HAROLD. Pardon?

INSPECTOR. Cuts, Mr Smith.

MAUREEN (*whispering urgently*). See — they're going to sever your frontal lobes.

HAROLD (*shouting*). You're not cutting me.

INSPECTOR. No, no — spending cuts. Government spending cuts. They're closing Redcar mental hospital.

MAUREEN (*shouting*). Well, they'll still extract his brains in Bradford.

HAROLD (*muttering*). Maybe I *should* jump out of the window.

MAUREEN. Harold.

INSPECTOR (*speaking slowly, as if to an idiot*). No need to panic, Mr Smith.

MAUREEN. You're not having him.

INSPECTOR. We don't want him, madam — not anymore. We're giving him to you . . . (*Slowly again:*) Do you understand, Mr Smith? The consultant has signed your release.

HAROLD. He's just told everybody I'm mad.

INSPECTOR. Quite — but madness no longer qualifies for a hospital bed. You can be just as mad in your own bed, which is cheaper. We call it community care. It enables the Government to employ more policemen to prevent you going mad in the street, where you might frighten the horses — that is, the police horses. Under new decrees on the 'privatisation of lunacy', madness is only permissible in private between consenting adults and at no cost to the Exchequer. So all I require now is your wife's consent.

HAROLD. To what?

INSPECTOR. Live with a madman.

MAUREEN. I consent.

INSPECTOR. Could you repeat that?

MAUREEN (*louder*). I consent.

INSPECTOR. In triplicate.

MAUREEN (*louder still*). I consent.

INSPECTOR. Excellent. All kidnapping charges against Maureen Smith and the Bradford and Bingley Brass Band are hereby withdrawn. Good-day.

Doors slam. The police siren is heard receding. The window bangs down.

Slowly, HAROLD *and* MAUREEN *begin to laugh, and laugh . . . then the laughter, too, fades away.*

MAUREEN (*finally*). Harold, you're free. It's all over.

HAROLD. No, love, it's just beginning.

On the trombone: witty, jaunty, the opening lines of 'Chatanooga Choo-choo'.

Silly beggars should have carved me up, while they'd chance. 'Cos King Canute's changing his tune. Swing with the tide, Your Majesty: there's enough spark in the sea to light up the whole world. And brother, are we gonna swing? We're gonna play with jazz bands, rock bands and reggae bands, colliery bands, sauce works bands, soul bands, salsa bands, rubber bands, harmonicas, flutes and flugelhorns, sitars, wobble-boards, any damned thing that makes the music, till we've found a song we can all play — and play it together, come hell or high water.

MAUREEN. Yes, Harold.

HAROLD. It's about time the Smiths called the tune in this bloody country.

MAUREEN. Yes. Yes. Yes.

On the trombone, the great theme from the last movement of Beethoven's Ninth Symphony. From all around, above and below, the whole band joins in to provide a boisterous, ringing 'Ode to Joy'.

THREE ATTEMPTED ACTS

by Martin Crimp

Martin Crimp was born in 1956, and lives in London with his wife and daughter. After leaving Cambridge University in 1978 he began to write fiction, producing a collection of short stories, *An Anatomy*, and a novel, *Still Early Days*, before becoming increasingly drawn to the possibilities of drama. Since 1980 he has had close links with the Orange Tree Theatre, Richmond, which has given first productions of *A Variety of Death-Defying Acts* (1985), and the one-woman show, *Living Remains* (1982), as well as an adaptation for stage of *Three Attempted Acts*, which is his first radio play. In his spare time he is a professional musician.

Three Attempted Acts was first broadcast on BBC Radio 3 on 15 May 1985. The cast was as follows:

MR LEBRUN }
MR DE A }   Alec McCowen
DR LEBRUN }

MRS COOK }
MRS LEBRUN }   Phyllida Law
MRS DE A }

BILLY   Mark Straker

Pianist: Martin Goldstein
Director: John Tydeman
Running time, as broadcast: 65 minutes 48 seconds.

1 The Appreciation of Music

MR LEBRUN. It was good of you to come at such short notice.

MRS COOK. It was good of you to invite me, Mr Lebrun. I tend to be
at something of a loss these evenings. (*Slight pause.*) You know you
sound quite different on the telephone.

MR LEBRUN. So I'm told, Mrs Cook.

Slight pause.

MRS COOK. Has there been any more trouble?

MR LEBRUN. Trouble?

MRS COOK. I thought there had been some . . . difficulties.

MR LEBRUN. Overcome, Mrs Cook. The difficulties as you call them
have been overcome.

MRS COOK. That's one in the eye for the sceptics.

MR LEBRUN. Not even worth discussing, Mrs Cook. Not worth the
breath.

MRS COOK. I know the sort.

MR LEBRUN. We can't all live in ivory towers.

MRS COOK. I beg your pardon, Mr Lebrun?

MR LEBRUN. The bible. The bible, Mrs Cook.

MRS COOK. Ah yes. Quite so. (*Pause.*) Jesus and so on. I know the sort,
believe you me. (*Pause.*)

MR LEBRUN. Shall we go through?

MRS COOK. Lead the way, Mr Lebrun.

Faint click of door as opened.

MR LEBRUN. After you.

> *Faint click of door as closed.*
> *Pause.*

MRS COOK. Well!

MR LEBRUN. What do you think?

MRS COOK. It's a very impressive arrangement, Mr Lebrun. Very impressive.

MR LEBRUN. I'm pleased you find it so.

MRS COOK. And is that our little prodigy over there in the straw?

MR LEBRUN. That's him, Mrs Cook.

MRS COOK. He doesn't look very perky.

MR LEBRUN. He's probably been exercising on his wheel. He has a passion for his wheel. He's probably worn himself out on it. It wouldn't be the first time.

MRS COOK. Has he got a name?

MR LEBRUN. Billy. His name is Billy.

MRS COOK (*enticing*). Hello, Billy . . . You've got a visitor . . . Billy . . . Billy . . . Wake up, Billy . . .

MR LEBRUN. Please keep your fingers this side of the mesh, Mrs Cook.

MRS COOK (*enticing*). Mr Lebrun's told me all about you . . . Who's a clever little thing . . . Who's a clever little thing . . . Billy . . . Billy . . .

> *Faint sound of movement in straw.*

I think he's waking up, Mr Lebrun. Billy . . . Billy . . .

> *More movement in straw.*

Well! Isn't he a fine specimen!

> *Movement in straw.*

He seems a little tangled in his tubes.

MR LEBRUN. He can sort himself out, Mrs Cook. The tubes come as second nature to him now.

MRS COOK. But there's one wrapped round his hindquarters.

MR LEBRUN. I'm sure he'll manage, Mrs Cook. Please keep your fingers this side of the mesh.

MRS COOK. I was only trying to help.

MR LEBRUN. It's a common enough response, but help is not something he appreciates. He can turn very nasty if you interfere.

MRS COOK. Is that so?

MR LEBRUN. He's not past biting the hand that feeds, Mrs Cook.

MRS COOK. Is that so? Shame. Shame on you, Billy.

MR LEBRUN. In fact I'm afraid he's a vicious little sod when all's said and done.

MRS COOK. Language, Mr Lebrun. Please! Shame on you. Shame on you both. (*Pause. She sniffs.*) It's rather close in here, don't you think? Perhaps we could open a window.

MR LEBRUN. I'm sorry but Billy here would most likely catch his death. I can't afford to have Billy catching his death.

MRS COOK. I realise that, Mr Lebrun, but —

MR LEBRUN. He's very sensitive to draughts.

MRS COOK. I daresay. It's just I'm beginning to feel a little —

MR LEBRUN. That's his anxiety I'm afraid.

MRS COOK. His anxiety? (*Slight pause.*)

MR LEBRUN. A by-product.

Pause. Sound of movement in straw.

MRS COOK. He's not in pain is he?

MR LEBRUN. What do you take me for, Mrs Cook?

MRS COOK. Suffering is one thing I can't abide.

MR LEBRUN. There's no question of suffering.

MRS COOK. It brings me out in a rash.

MR LEBRUN. It's a common enough response.

MRS COOK. But it can last for hours.

MR LEBRUN. You should see a doctor.

MRS COOK. I have. (*Pause.*) No pain then?

MR LEBRUN. You have my word.

MRS COOK. And the window . . .

MR LEBRUN. I have to act in Billy's best interests, Mrs Cook.

Pause. Movement in the straw.

MRS COOK. Billy . . . You know I think it suits him. He looks like a Billy. Was it your idea to call him that, Mr Lebrun?

MR LEBRUN. Well, it was hardly his mother's, was it?

Slight pause. He begins to laugh.

MRS COOK. (*After a moment joins in the laughter.*) Oh, Mr Lebrun you are terrible! His mother . . . Whatever next? (*Laughter ends.*) And to think I've always thought of you as rather dour. (*Pronounced 'dower'.*)

MR LEBRUN. I think dour (*like 'tour'.*) is the word, Mrs Cook. I think you mean you've always thought of me as rather dour.

Pause.

MRS COOK. Why's he looking at me like that?

MR LEBRUN. He must imagine you were laughing at *him*, Mrs Cook. He's not fond of being laughed at.

MRS COOK. He's certainly quick to take umbrage.

MR LEBRUN. He doesn't like being laughed at, that's all.

MRS COOK. I wasn't laughing at you, Billy. I was laughing at Mr Lebrun.

MR LEBRUN. I'm afraid it brings out the worst in him.

MRS COOK. But I meant no harm.

Movement in the straw.

MR LEBRUN. Well since he's perked up I think we can put him through his paces now, don't you?

Faint metallic sounds accompany the following passage.

The structure in front of his nose is the bar.

MRS COOK. The bar . . .

MR LEBRUN. The bar is connected by these rods to the food hopper . . .

MRS COOK. The food hopper . . .

MR LEBRUN. Which is in turn connected to the green tube . . .

MRS COOK. The green tube . . .

MR LEBRUN. Which as you can see leads to the galvanised trough.

MRS COOK. Ah yes, the galvanised trough.

Pause.

It's most impressive, Mr Lebrun.

MR LEBRUN. We haven't begun yet, Mrs Cook. The bar must first be released electrically.

Sound of switch thrown, followed by movement in the straw. Then the sound of the metal bar being depressed, a slight pause, then the sound of a mouth at the trough for three seconds. Then again sound of bar depressed, slight pause, sound of mouth at trough for three seconds. This cycle of sounds continues steadily while they speak.

MRS COOK. But Mr Lebrun, it's quite remarkable!

MR LEBRUN. Thank you. As you can see, whenever our Billy here presses down on the bar, (*Sound of bar.*) he initiates a temporary and measured flow of food from the food hopper, via the green tube, into the galvanised trough.

Sound of mouth at trough.

MRS COOK. I honestly wouldn't have believed it possible.

MR LEBRUN. You have to see it with your own eyes, Mrs Cook.

MRS COOK. But how on earth did he manage to grasp the principle?

MR LEBRUN. Trial, Mrs Cook. Trial, and error.

Sounds continue.

This can go on almost indefinitely.

MRS COOK. The food in the trough then . . . is his reward as it were . . . for pressing down on the bar.

Sounds continue.

MR LEBRUN. You could look at it that way.

MRS COOK. What is the food?

MR LEBRUN. Nothing out of the ordinary, Mrs Cook. The only criterion is that it should pass freely through the tube.

MRS COOK. It's remarkable.

Sounds continue.

Have you ever wondered what would happen if you stopped the supply?

MR LEBRUN. I see you have an enquiring mind, Mrs Cook. I was coming to that . . .

Sound of mouth at trough. Sound of a tap being turned. Sound of bar depressed. Pause. Bar depressed. Shorter pause. Bar depressed once more, then again, then again and again with increasing agitation.

This can go on almost indefinitely.

MRS COOK. How extraordinary. Doesn't he understand the food has stopped?

MR LEBRUN. I wouldn't like to say, Mrs Cook. It all depends what you mean by understand.

Repeated banging of bar.

MRS COOK. But he's quite beside himself. Billy, Billy, stop that!

MR LEBRUN. I warned you about his nasty moods.

Repeated banging of bar.

MRS COOK. Perhaps we should start the food again.

Repeated banging of bar.

MR LEBRUN. In one sense of course he totally fails to understand.

Yet in another one might say he understands only too well. Don't you, Billy?

Repeated banging of bar.

MRS COOK (*with emphasis*). Could you not start the food again please, Mr Lebrun?

MR LEBRUN. But of course.

Faint sound of tap being turned. Banging of bar ceases. Sound of mouth at trough as before. Bar then depressed as before. Cycle of sounds begins and continues steadily as before.

MRS COOK (*tentatively*). I wonder, Mr Lebrun . . . I wonder have you ever found yourself asking if what you're doing is . . . quite right?

MR LEBRUN. I beg your pardon? (*Slight pause.*) I beg your pardon?

MRS COOK. What I mean is is have you never found yourself wondering — perhaps in your more . . . reflective moments — wondering whether it may be wrong to spend all your time here with Billy in this way . . . and never —

MR LEBRUN. I'm sorry I'm not with you, Mrs Cook.

MRS COOK. What I mean is is I for my part at least have started to enrol or perhaps it would be more accurate to say I have started to investigate the possibility of enrolling for courses, one course that is in particular.

MR LEBRUN. Courses?

MRS COOK. An educational course, Mr Lebrun. I have started to think quite seriously about the possibility of enrolling for an educational course in music.

MR LEBRUN. Congratulations, Mrs Cook! I must say it's most courageous to take up an instrument at your time of life.

MRS COOK. Not quite an instrument, Mr Lebrun. I'm not sure I'd be quite up to an instrument as of yet. No, I was thinking more for the time being in terms of appreciation. The appreciation of music I mean.

Sounds continue.

With perhaps an instrument later, when the appreciation was mastered. Because to tell the truth, Mr Lebrun, I have very little appreciation of music at the moment. I find it irksome at the best of times. And at the worst I have a kind of loathing for it. Which is why I would like to educate and improve myself in that respect, the musical respect. Since I'm not at all sure this loathing can be quite natural. And besides I thought that simply to enrol for a course, any course, might give me the chance, might give me some kind of chance to . . .

Pause. Cycle of bar and mouth at trough continues.

MRS COOK. So you see what I meant was really to ask if ever you had had similar . . . yearnings.

Pause. Sounds continue.

I realise of course it's none of my business.

Pause. Sounds continue.

I meant no harm, Mr Lebrun.

Pause. Sounds continue.

Well, I must say our Billy here has certainly grasped the principle. It's quite remarkable.

MR LEBRUN. A life's work, Mrs Cook.

MRS COOK. I can imagine.

MR LEBRUN. It has not been without its difficulties.

MRS COOK. I can well imagine.

Pause. Mouth at trough.

MR LEBRUN. I think we could go on to the next stage now.

MRS COOK. Do you mean there's more, Mr Lebrun?

Faint sound of switch thrown. Immediately following the next depression of the bar is the sound of a violent movement in the straw.

Good lord! What was that?

Pause, then sound of mouth at trough.

Was it electricity, Mr Lebrun?

Mouth finishes at trough. Bar pressed again. Immediately another violent movement in the straw. Longer pause, then sound of mouth at trough.

Is it electricity in the bar, Mr Lebrun? Isn't that dangerous?

Mouth finishes at trough. Silence.

What's he going to do?

Violent depression of bar immediately followed by the violent movement.

MRS COOK. Isn't electricity dangerous?

MR LEBRUN. Not if you've done your sums, Mrs Cook.

Sound of mouth at trough.

You don't embark upon a project of this magnitude without doing your sums.

MRS COOK. He doesn't seem deterred.

MR LEBRUN. Not for the moment, no.

> *Once more a violent depression of the bar followed by the violent movement.*

MRS COOK. He's going to do himself an injury if he's not careful.

> *Sounds of mouth at trough. Mouth finishes at trough.*
> *Silence.*

MR LEBRUN (*intense*). There . . . You see how the situation has changed. He wants to fill his trough again and as we are both well aware he knows that to fill his trough he simply has to press down on the bar. But now you see, in the light of his most recent experiences, he has also come to understand for want of a better word that if he presses down on the bar —

MRS COOK. He'll be electrocuted.

MR LEBRUN. You've grasped it, Mrs Cook.

MRS COOK. But what'll he do?

> *Silence.*

What's he going to do, Mr Lebrun?

> *Silence.*

I can't bear the suspense.

> *Silence.*

MR LEBRUN. Pay close attention, Mrs Cook. Pay close attention . . . There!

> *Faint movement in the straw.*

MRS COOK. Good lord!

MR LEBRUN. You see. It never fails.

MRS COOK. But can't he help himself?

MR LEBRUN. Once he's started he can go on almost indefinitely.

MRS COOK. But why? Why does he do it?

MR LEBRUN. It's given me sleepless nights, Mrs Cook, believe you me. But in the end I've come to the conclusion it must be anxiety. A by-product of his anxiety.

MRS COOK. But why's he anxious? What reason has he to be anxious?

MR LEBRUN. It's a mystery to me too, Mrs Cook. I still can't fathom it.

MRS COOK. It's remarkable. I'd never have believed it unless I'd seen it with my own eyes.

MR LEBRUN. All things must be seen, Mrs Cook, before they can be believed.

MRS COOK. There's absolutely no control.

MR LEBRUN. No attempt at control. That's the astonishing part. He doesn't even try.

Pause. Faint movement in the straw.

MRS COOK. Should we find him a rag?

MR LEBRUN. A rag, Mrs Cook? Whatever would he do with a rag?

MRS COOK. Why's he looking at us like that?

MR LEBRUN. He probably thinks we're laughing at him.

MRS COOK. But why should he think that?

MR LEBRUN. He's not fond of being laughed at.

MRS COOK. But why should he think that? We're not laughing. We're not laughing at you, Billy. We're not laughing at all. Why is he looking at us like that?

BILLY *begins to speak. He makes loud, unintelligible, but clearly human sounds, like the unformed syllables of a deaf-mute.*

BILLY. Mmm . . . ba . . . bah . . . berr . . . mag . . . ga . . . ga . . . geer . . . bah . . . fer . . . fer . . .

Sounds continue.

MRS COOK. What's he saying, Mr Lebrun?

BILLY. . . . brr . . . mma . . . mmu . . . ga . . . gra . . .

MRS COOK. What's he saying? Is he talking to us?

BILLY. . . . berr . . . mag . . . mag . . . ler . . . ler . . .

MR LEBRUN. Your guess is as good as mine, Mrs Cook.

BILLY. . . . frr . . . brr . . . fer . . . mma . . . mmu . . . ga . . .

MRS COOK. But what does it mean?

MR LEBRUN. It never lasts.

BILLY. . . . ler . . . ler . . . grrla . . . mma . . . mmer . . . agat . . .

MRS COOK. What is it, Billy? Do you want to tell us something?

BILLY (*continues speaking*).

MRS COOK (*a sudden idea*). Perhaps he's trying to tell us why he's anxious, Mr Lebrun.

MR LEBRUN (*laughs*). It's certainly a charming idea, but I'm afraid it's unlikely. Very unlikely. To be frank, it's most probably abuse.

BILLY. . . . mma . . . ssha . . . ssha . . . ga . . . ffa . . . ffer . . .

MRS COOK. Abuse?

MR LEBRUN. Verbal abuse, Mrs Cook.

BILLY. . . . mma . . . ffa . . . ffa . . . grr . . . grra . . . ssho . . .

MRS COOK. I wish you hadn't told me that, Mr Lebrun. Language is one thing I can't abide.

BILLY (*continues*).

MRS COOK. Make him stop.

BILLY (*continues*).

MRS COOK. Make him stop.

BILLY (*continues*).

MRS COOK. Please make him stop!

BILLY (*continues for several seconds before his voice dies away*).

Silence.

MRS COOK. Language is one thing I simply cannot abide, you see. It brings me out in a rash. At the first hint. A great red rash. You wouldn't believe the prurience of it. (*Pause.*) Would it not be possible to open a window, Mr Lebrun? Just a tiny way? (*Pause.*) Well. It's certainly one in the eye for the sceptics and no mistake. If they could only come and see your Billy . . . in the flesh . . . Since I'm sure I don't need to tell you that there are some who take — I hesitate to call it dim — but blinkered perhaps, yes, who take a blinkered view of how things stand. I'm sure I don't need to tell you that.

Pause. Faint metallic sounds.

So. You must have things to do. I mustn't keep you from your work. I'm so glad I came. I'm so often at a loss in the evenings.

Pause. Faint metallic sounds.

You know . . . I think I would like to begin with Mozart. I mean all those tunes, those melodies of his! It's quite exquisite. The pain I mean, Mr Lebrun, the exquisite pain of it. You just wouldn't believe how those melodies probe my nerves. It's like a needle, Mr Lebrun, a needle next to the bone. Sheer torment. A moment's Mozart and I'm at screaming pitch before I know where I am. That's the effect those melodies have. Quite intolerable. And so I tell myself that if I could only learn to appreciate those melodies I could appreciate anything. That's how I reason. If I could listen to one of those melodies for only a moment without the usual suffering I tell myself the rest of music would be child's play. Don't you think?

MR LEBRUN. It's certainly possible, Mrs Cook. Though I must admit I've never had any trouble with melodies myself. No, as far as I'm concerned the harmonies have always been the sticking point.

Pause.

MRS COOK. Harmonies? I'm afraid I'm not quite with you.

Pause.

What are the harmonies, Mr Lebrun?

The music for the next Act begins almost immediately.

2 Making Love

The slow movement of Mozart's Piano Concerto in A (K488) begins. The music sounds remote and tinny. After the first four bars, there are close, faint gasps from MRS LEBRUN, *and* MR DE A *begins to speak. The gasps continue erratically and are audible whenever* MR DE A *falls silent. It should be evident from* MR DE A*'s manner of speaking that he is simultaneously concentrating on another task.*

MR DE A. I very much suspect, Mrs Lebrun, there will be a frost tonight. Quite possibly it will mean the end of my beans.

MRS LEBRUN (*gasps*).

Music.

MR DE A. Sometimes I ask myself if it's worth all the effort.

MRS LEBRUN (*gasps*).

Music continues.

MR DE A. Since I've already been caught out once by the cold snap earlier on in the year, and what with the possibility of an early frost now . . . I'm beginning to have my doubts about vegetables. . . . If you could just turn a little, Mrs Lebrun. Yes, that's right. Turn a little. That's much better. . . . And of course they were stringy to begin with, and then, towards the end of the season, they turned woody. Do you know, I've hardly had one edible bean all year, Mrs Lebrun. . . . Relax, Mrs Lebrun. . . . Some years give the impression of lacking a summer, don't you think? It seems no sooner have the buds broken than the leaves are falling. Have you noticed?

MRS LEBRUN (*gasps*).

Music continues.

MR DE A. If you could just turn a little more. That's right. Turn . . . And relax. Good. We're doing splendidly. . . . Not every year, I hasten to add. Since I've known some long summers, Mrs Lebrun, some terribly long summers. There are times when I've looked at my potatoes and just wanted to weep.

MRS LEBRUN (*loud gasp*).

MR DE A. That wasn't painful was it, Mrs Lebrun?

MRS LEBRUN. . . . uh . . . uh . . .

MR DE A. Try and concentrate on the music. It will help you relax . . . What's your opinion of sweet peas? Do you know if they're easy from seed?

MRS LEBRUN (*louder gasp*).

MR DE A. Is the music not helping?

MRS LEBRUN. . . . na . . . na . . . (*The gasps diminish.*)

*Sound of steel instruments set down on enamel surface.
The music stops.*

MR DE A. That's a pity, Mrs Lebrun. Usually I find the music a great success with the ladies. They seem more susceptible as a rule.

MRS LEBRUN. I daresay, Mr de A. But to be frank, I'd sooner be unconscious. I used to prefer that arrangement.

MR DE A. Well yes, a few years ago it's true I would've put you under without the least pause, but recently you see I've come to believe the important thing is that you should feel what I'm doing, and be able to respond. In that way I become more appreciative of your personal requirements.

MRS LEBRUN. But the pain . . .

MR DE A. I can assure you, Mrs Lebrun, the pain was far worse when you didn't feel it. Technically speaking. Isn't that so, Lucy? You wouldn't believe the damage we used to do in all innocence when there was no response. A clean probe please, Lucy.

MRS LEBRUN. What happened to the other one, Mr de A?

Sound of steel instruments set down on enamel.

MR DE A. Thank you, Lucy. What other one is that? Open please.

MRS LEBRUN (*with open mouth, almost unintelligible*). Yvonne. What happened to Yvonne?

MR DE A (*concentrating as at first*). Yvonne is no longer with us, Mrs Lebrun.

MRS LEBRUN (*with open mouth*). I used to like Yvonne.

MR DE A. Just turn a little please . . . That's right . . .

MRS LEBRUN (*sudden loud gasp*).

MR DE A. Really, Mrs Lebrun, if the probe gives you so much trouble, heaven alone knows what you will make of the drill.

MRS LEBRUN (*with open mouth*). The drill?

Sound of steel instruments set down on enamel.

(*Normal voice.*) The drill, Mr de A?

I did so love the gas. I had such wonderful dreams with that gas. Don't you do the gas any more?

MR DE A. It's only a small cavity, Mrs Lebrun.

MRS LEBRUN. Perhaps I should have a jab then.

MR DE A. A jab? Are you taking any drugs?

MRS LEBRUN. Only my pills, Mr de A.

MR DE A. What sort of pills?

MRS LEBRUN. The green ones. I take the green ones for my anxiety. And the red ones for my skin. The green ones bring my skin out in a rash, you see.

MR DE A. In that case, Mrs Lebrun, a jab is quite out of the question. You wouldn't want us to be responsible for putting you into a coma, would you? Could we have a clean bib for Mrs Lebrun please, Lucy.

MRS LEBRUN. Where is Yvonne these days then?

MR DE A. Thank you, Lucy. She has a charming smile don't you think?

MRS LEBRUN (*gasps*).

MR DE A. What is it, Mrs Lebrun?

MRS LEBRUN (*strangled*). She's tying it too tightly, Mr de A.

MR DE A. Loosen the bib a little, Lucy. That's right. We must take care of our patient. Don't be too harsh on her, Mrs Lebrun. Perhaps I shouldn't tell you this, but I took her on without any previous dental experience at all. Her qualities were just too obvious to ignore. And besides, there is such a thing as too much experience, don't you agree? Is that more comfortable?

MRS LEBRUN. I suppose so.

MR DE A. She's really very sensitive to a patient's requirements.

MRS LEBRUN. I've no doubt, Mr de A.

MR DE A. She hates suffering of any kind, Mrs Lebrun. She used to work with animals you know. (*Pause.*) Shall we try the music again?

MRS LEBRUN. Yvonne was such a pleasant girl.

MR DE A. She may have appeared so, Mrs Lebrun.

MRS LEBRUN. What do you mean?

MR DE A. She may have appeared to be a pleasant girl. In fact we all believed that she was. But events proved us wrong.

MRS LEBRUN. Events, Mr de A?

MR DE A. There was an incident, Mrs Lebrun. In the waiting-room. Open please.

MRS LEBRUN. What kind of incident?

MR DE A. Open please. That's splendid.

MRS LEBRUN (*with open mouth*). What kind of incident, Mr de A?

Whine of high-speed drill.

MR DE A. If you should experience any pain, Mrs Lebrun, just raise your hand.

Whine of high-speed drill, fluctuating in pitch.

MRS LEBRUN (*her gasps become more intense*).

Drill ceases. Fifteen seconds in all.

MR DE A. Was that causing you pain?

MRS LEBRUN. I had raised my hand, Mr de A.

MR DE A. I'm sorry, I didn't realise it was intentional. I took it for a reflex. Would you like a rinse now. Have a rinse, Mrs Lebrun, and then we can review the situation.

Sound of chair ascending electrically.

I'm tempted to give up vegetables altogether. Lucy here says I should have a go at flowers for a change. She has a passion for flowers.

MRS LEBRUN. I thought it was animals, Mr de A. (*She spits.*)

MR DE A. She has a passion for all God's creations, Mrs Lebrun. She says that come spring we should grow sweet peas up over the window, and take down the Venetian blind. It's a charming idea don't you think?

MRS LEBRUN (*spits*).

MR DE A. The everlasting variety.

MRS LEBRUN (*spits at length*).

MR DE A. Now, shall we have another look at that tooth?

Sound of chair descending, and of dental instruments.

Open please. A little more.

(*Concentrating as at first.*) I must admit, Mrs Lebrun, I had assumed you would know about the incident with Yvonne. . . . Turn my way a little. Thank you. . . . You know how word gets about. Of course it was several months ago now.

MRS LEBRUN (*faint gasps audible as at first*).

MR DE A. If you came for more regular treatment, dare I say it, you would be a little better informed into the bargain. . . . Of course, it might never have happened if there had been more people in the waiting-room at the time. It was the end of surgery, you see. And I was a little behind schedule. I'd run into difficulties with an abscess.

Short burst of high-pressure air-jet.

MRS LEBRUN (*gasps*).

MR DE A. It's only air, Mrs Lebrun.

Pause.

Yes . . . I'm afraid we'll have to go a little deeper. . . . Don't look so alarmed, Mrs Lebrun. If you saw some of the cavities that came in here you'd know when you were well off, believe you me. . . . Would you like Lucy to hold your hand? She has a very comforting hand. Lucy, will you hold Mrs Lebrun's hand, please.

MRS LEBRUN. I'm not a child, Mr de A.

MR DE A. Don't be embarrassed, Mrs Lebrun. There are plenty of grown men who couldn't do without Lucy's hand. Open please.

Whine of high-speed drill, fluctuating in pitch.

MRS LEBRUN (*as before her faint gasps become more intense*). . . .

. . . *until the drill finally ceases. (Twenty seconds in all.)*

MR DE A. Well done, Mrs Lebrun! That was very brave.

MRS LEBRUN. I was going to raise my hand, Mr de A.

MR DE A. But you overcame the urge. That's splendid.

MRS LEBRUN. She was holding it down.

MR DE A. Sorry?

MRS LEBRUN. Your nurse. She was holding down my hand.

MR DE A. But I asked her to hold your hand, Mrs Lebrun.

MRS LEBRUN. Not both of them, Mr de A. Not both of them.

Pause.

MR DE A. You can let go of Mrs Lebrun's hands now, Lucy. Rinse please.

Sound of chair ascending.

(*Somewhat rhetorical:*) My own view, Mrs Lebrun, and I don't wish this to sound pompous, but my own view is that humanity as a whole is rather over-addicted to anaesthesia.

MRS LEBRUN (*spits*).

MR DE A. And I don't merely mean anaesthesia of the body, since would you not agree that there is also such a thing as an anaesthesia of the spirit, an anaesthesia, if I may make so bold, of the soul?

MRS LEBRUN (*spits*). Should there be blood, Mr de A?

MR DE A (*normal voice*). I'd be worried if there wasn't, Mrs Lebrun. (*Rhetorical:*) You may mock me as much as you like, but I've given the matter some thought over the years, some considerable thought. And I have come to the conclusion that we are all of us in danger of succumbing to a numbness from which we may never recover, a kind of frost-bite as it were, in the heart.

MRS LEBRUN (*spits*).

MR DE A. How else, Mrs Lebrun, can we explain man's manifest indifference to man?

MRS LEBRUN. I really can't imagine, Mr de A. (*She spits.*)

MR DE A. And really indifference is too weak a word, since what are we to make of those people who actively provoke and prolong the suffering of their fellow creatures, either in the name of reason, or quite simply for their own pleasure? They are a very strange case don't you think? But not at all rare — on the contrary. Common humanity, Mrs Lebrun, common humanity is much less common than the name implies. Since there was a time, and correct me if I'm wrong but I'm sure you will agree that there was undoubtedly a time when it was more important to suffer than to bring about suffering, suffer that is not just on one's own behalf but for others, Mrs Lebrun, for others, that was the beauty of it. But now I'm afraid one glance round my waiting-room is enough to convince me that people have lost the knack. They just wouldn't know where to begin. Oh they may whine and whimper in this chair but the truth is they couldn't suffer if they tried. They're numb, Mrs Lebrun, already quite numb. Nothing I could give would deaden them any further.

Sound of chair descending.

MRS LEBRUN. Yes. (*Slight pause.*) Do tell me about the waiting-room, Mr de A.

MR DE A. That's quite another matter. That was a different business entirely. Open please.

Sound of instruments etc.

(*Concentrating as at first.*) As I was saying, it was the end of surgery, or very nearly the end. I was dealing with a rather nasty abscess at the time and my last client of the day was still in the waiting-room.

MRS LEBRUN (*faint gasps audible as at first*).

MR DE A. Close a little. Thank you. . . . Petley his name was, a Mr Petley. He'd come to have his new dentures fitted. I'd removed what remained of his teeth some weeks earlier. If he possessed a toothbrush, I doubt if it had ever seen the inside of his mouth, in which case the toothbrush was very fortunate. . . . Mr Petley was very anxious to have his dentures fitted at the earliest possible date, since when I had completed the extractions, owing to the rather peculiar anatomy of his maxilla, I had been unable to find a suitable set of dentures to tide him over until his own had been made. I think he was rather worried about the consequences to his social activity.

Burst of air-jet as before.

MRS LEBRUN (*gasps*).

MR DE A. Well we're down to the nerve, Mrs Lebrun. I don't think we need go any further you'll be pleased to hear. Lining please, Lucy.

Sound of dental instruments as appropriate.

MRS LEBRUN (*gasps faintly audible as before*).

MR DE A. Thank you, Lucy. I really don't know how I ever managed without her, Mrs Lebrun. When I look back now I realise that in the past this practice was dogged by inefficiency and God only knows what else to an extent I had never even guessed at. . . . Anyway, Mr Petley was due in at quarter past four and he'd arrived at ten past evidently. At about half past four I realised that I'd bitten off rather more than I'd expected to chew with the abscess and so I sent Yvonne into the waiting-room to advise Mr Petley of this state of affairs, and warn him that he might yet have some while to wait. . . . Just close a little more. Splendid. Amalgam please, Lucy. . . . I had naturally expected Yvonne to return immediately and continue assisting me. To be frank I had rather hoped that she might manage to use some tact and persuade Mr Petley to go home and make an appointment for the following day, despite his obvious need. . . . Thank you, Lucy. I never have to ask her for anything twice. It's quite miraculous. It's almost as if she anticipates one's requirements don't you think? . . . But the next thing I knew, you see, Mrs Cook, another of my clients, came running in here saying that I should go into the waiting-room at once. You can imagine the scene I'm sure. There I was, in the middle of a tricky incision, and one of my clients, who didn't even have an appointment by the way, comes rushing in without any warning.

Sound of amalgam squeezed into tooth, etc.

This Mrs Cook, you see, as I later discovered, had developed a severe toothache earlier in the day, and had come along hoping to persuade me to see her after hours. She was agitated beyond all reason. . . . Open a little more please.

Sounds of treatment as appropriate.

That's splendid. . . . Well, of course, under such unusual circumstances I felt I had no choice but to abandon my patient and comply with Mrs Cook's request to go to the waiting-room. . . . You wouldn't believe, Mrs Lebrun, what was taking place in there.

MRS LEBRUN (*with open mouth, almost unintelligible*). What was it?

MR DE A. Hold still please. I haven't finished yet. The magazines, Mrs Lebrun, the magazines were all over the floor. And in one corner of the room, to the left of the fireplace, Yvonne was . . . reclining, with Mr Petley on top of her.

MRS LEBRUN (*with open mouth*). Uh!

MR DE A. Without his teeth, Mrs Lebrun. Remember that. Without his teeth. It was a disgusting scene. It revealed an aspect of Yvonne's character that I had previously been blind to, completely blind. Since Mr Petley was almost a complete stranger to her, and only ten minutes had elapsed since I sent her in to him. Only ten minutes, yes. I looked at the clock. It turned my stomach, Mrs Lebrun, you can imagine. And as for the look in her eyes, it was pure oblivion.

Treatment continues.

Pure oblivion, Mrs Lebrun, there's no other word. As if Mr Petley was
a gift from heaven. . . . Well, the moment he realised I was in the
room he was off like a shot, wasn't he? The embarrassment you see.
He barged past Mrs Cook and myself without so much as a by your
leave. . . . But at least he had the good grace to go, because as for
Yvonne, she simply lay there, quite unashamed. She made no attempt
to make herself decent. She just lay there with her head on the hearth.
Mrs Cook and I had to haul her to her feet and manoeuvre her into
a chair. Bite please, Mrs Lebrun.

MRS LEBRUN (*normal voice*). Are you saying the man was trying to
rape her, Mr de A? Did you call for the police?

MR DE A. Bite please, Mrs Lebrun.

MRS LEBRUN (*snaps her teeth together*).

MR DE A. Can you feel anything?

MRS LEBRUN. It's not quite even. So this . . . Petley was a rapist . . .
How terrible for Yvonne.

MR DE A. Open please.

He begins to scrape at excess amalgam.

It seems that I have inadvertently given you an erroneous impression
of events, Mrs Lebrun. Since I can assure you that there was no
question here of unwillingness. That's a very novel interpretation
I must say. . . . Did I not mention her look was one of oblivion?
And would it not be a reasonable supposition that in a case of the
kind you suggest her look would most likely be one of anguish?
I think, Mrs Lebrun, that the difference between anguish and oblivion
is a perfectly clear one, don't you? Besides I heard no struggle. Surely
in a case of the kind you suggest a struggle is obligatory? Bite please.

MRS LEBRUN (*snaps her teeth together*). But what about the
magazines, Mr de A?

MR DE A. A number of them were quite ruined, I'm afraid.

MRS LEBRUN. But weren't the scattered magazines evidence of a
struggle?

MR DE A. Hardly. I think you will find that poor Mr Petley, tired of
waiting for his dentures, had decided to amuse himself by looking
through the magazines, and finding nothing to his taste — since as
you know the majority of the magazines are the ladies' kind —
expressed his displeasure and passed the time by making a mess of
them. Rather childish I agree, but these things happen. How is it
now, Mrs Lebrun?

MRS LEBRUN (*with irritation*). It's far from perfect, Mr de A.

MR DE A (*still working at the tooth*). And of course the gasping puts the
matter beyond any shadow of a doubt. Did I mention the gasping?
Because you see she was gasping for all she was worth, surely proof

if any further proof were needed of her complicity not to mention
her impending satisfaction.

MRS LEBRUN (*vehement*). But surely it was the pain.

MR DE A. Pain, Mrs Lebrun? What pain is that? I think you'll find it
level now. Can you bite again please. (*Slight pause.*) Bite please.

MRS LEBRUN (*vehement*). I mean her fear, Mr de A. Her pain and
her fear.

MR DE A. Please bite, Mrs Lebrun, or we'll never finish.

MRS LEBRUN (*snaps her teeth together*).

MR DE A. Is it satisfactory?

MRS LEBRUN (*with irritation*). Yes thank you.

MR DE A. That's splendid then. Of course I would be the first to agree
that in a case of the kind you have suggested gasps of pain or distress
would most certainly be the general rule. But these were quite clearly
gasps of pleasure, Mrs Lebrun.

MRS LEBRUN (*vehement*). But how can you distinguish, Mr de A?
How can you distinguish?

Long pause.

MR DE A. A final rinse then.

Sound of chair ascending.

Lucy, some more mouthwash for Mrs Lebrun please. You've gone
quite white, Mrs Lebrun. You're not suffering are you? The tooth's
not reacting is it?

MRS LEBRUN *is silent.*

If you should have any trouble with it you only have to call by. But
in general we've found that complications have grown much rarer
since we stopped indiscriminate anaesthesia. The benefits have been
enormous on both sides.

Sound of glass set down on enamel surface.

Thank you, Lucy. Don't you think she's doing terribly well,
Mrs Lebrun? I'm really very pleased with Lucy's progress. And
I don't think we're going to run into the same kind of . . . snag
with her, do you? Because there's such an air of innocence about
her, don't you think?

MRS LEBRUN (*spits*).

MR DE A. And I don't just mean the innocence of a child, which after all
is a very dubious notion to my mind, but more the innocence of an
animal wouldn't you say, or even of a flower.

MRS LEBRUN (*spits*).

MR DE A. Would you like a tissue, Mrs Lebrun? Lucy, fetch Mrs Lebrun a tissue. That's right. She has such a charming smile, don't you think? (*Pause.*) Mr Petley's most impressed. He says he's never seen such an angel. He says now his new teeth have settled in they've transformed his social life beyond all recognition. They've opened doors at every level of society evidently. He's out most evenings moving in circles he'd never even dreamt of, visiting the theatre, learning to appreciate the popular classics. And he says the credit's entirely mine. Or ours I should say. He says the credit is entirely ours. You know it's really very gratifying, Mrs Lebrun, when something like that happens.

3. Suicide

The sound of MRS DE A *humming to herself. She is humming her own somewhat inaccurate version of the opening theme of Mozart's Piano Sonata in A, (K331). She is interrupted by a buzzer. Faint footsteps follow, then the sound of a deadlock, and of a door opened as far as a chain permits.*

MRS DE A. Yes?

DR LEBRUN. My name's Lebrun, Doctor Lebrun. I'm looking for a Mrs de A.

Door immediately slammed. Faint fiddling with the chain.
Door opened fully.

MRS DE A. Doctor! Come in! I must admit, we were beginning to think you'd forgotten us.

Door shut and locked.

DR LEBRUN. Hardly that, Mrs de A. Hardly that. I simply spent more time than I had foreseen in the lift.

MRS DE A. Yes, that lift. It doesn't like stopping at the sixteenth floor for some reason. For some reason it always continues right to the top of the building.

DR LEBRUN. So I found, Mrs de A.

MRS DE A. Right to the top. And there it stays more often than not I'm afraid. You didn't resort to the alarm did you?

DR LEBRUN. The doors came open of their own accord after a while.

MRS DE A. You were well advised to wait. Personally I wouldn't touch that alarm again if you paid me. Once bitten, Doctor. Once bitten.

DR LEBRUN. It was no trouble to make my way back down the stairs.

MRS DE A. It brings the porter you know.

DR LEBRUN. I'm not averse to moderate exercise.

MRS DE A. He comes down the shaft and makes his way in through a little hatch, would you believe. (*Slight pause.*) Of course the piano came up in the service lift. There's never any trouble with the service lift.

DR LEBRUN. It looks a splendid instrument.

MRS DE A. It's the concert model, Doctor. We paid for it out of the insurance. I took her down to Cook's to choose it the moment the insurance came through. It's a white one, of course. I've never liked dark furniture, have you? Do you know Cook's?

DR LEBRUN. I don't think so.

MRS DE A. Of course it's not what it was. Rose wept for days the poor darling. Tears of gratitude you understand. She's a very emotional child.

DR LEBRUN. Emotional intensity is a natural concomitant of musical precociousness, Mrs de A.

MRS DE A. You took the words out of my mouth, Doctor.

DR LEBRUN. And when are we going to have the pleasure of hearing your daughter play?

MRS DE A. Whenever you wish. She's been in her bedroom all morning studying the music. (*She calls:*) Rose! Rose, the doctor's here. (*Normal voice:*) She always studies the music before she performs.

DR LEBRUN. She seems to have a very adult approach.

MRS DE A. Adult? I'd hardly call it that. Adult is not a word we like to use here. It stinks of marriage and mediocrity, don't you think? But you could certainly call her approach a professional one, and undoubtedly determined, because Rose has always been a terribly determined girl. She began to play when she was three years old you know, and since then there's never been the least hesitation, never any piece she couldn't just take in her stride.

DR LEBRUN. And has she never had any trouble with the stretches?

MRS DE A. The stretches, Doctor? What do you mean, the stretches?

DR LEBRUN. Intervals, Mrs de A. Stretching intervals. Of course you know that wonderful story about Mozart, don't you? Whether it's true or not is another matter. But they say that the little Mozart, who like your daughter, began to play music almost the moment he saw the light of day, they say that when he came to certain stretches his infant hands couldn't manage, he would supply the missing note with his nose. (*He laughs.*) It's a charming idea, isn't it? (*He laughs a little more.*)

Silence.

MRS DE A. Rose has never played with her nose, Doctor Lebrun. She has always used her fingers. She's not a variety act. She plays the piano in the normal way.

DR LEBRUN. The story's probably a complete fabrication.

MRS DE A. My daughter is not a freak, Doctor.

DR LEBRUN. Of course not, Mrs de A. (*Pause.*) I take it you yourself are musical?

MRS DE A. I can appreciate the beauty of music, Doctor, the sublime radiance of the sounds. Whenever Rose plays I feel my soul open up to the light, the light simply pours in, you can't imagine. But of course I'm not a musician in what you would call the active sense of the word. That wouldn't suit me at all. All those exercises . . . All that study . . . Out of the question I'm afraid. Now my husband on the other hand, Mr de A, whatever faults he may've had, his was certainly a considerable talent. Yes, my word, what an organ that man had.

DR LEBRUN. He sang?

MRS DE A. At parties, Doctor. They'd never let him leave till he'd performed. That's how I met him actually. (*Slight pause.*) He would probably have done you one of his numbers, only he ruined his voice, and he's dead of course. (*Slight pause.*) It was his anxiety, you see. It was in his bones. It oozed, Doctor, from the man's marrow. His anxiety that is. He jumped from that window by the piano and impaled himself on the Admiral Spitz memorial. (*She calls.*) Rose! Come along, Rose! (*Normal voice.*) Apparently a distance of some fifty-three metres. (*She calls:*) Rose! The Doctor's waiting. He hasn't got all day.

DR LEBRUN. It's tragic, Mrs de A.

MRS DE A. There were days I swear you could see him oozing, actually see him.

DR LEBRUN. It must have been a terrible shock for you both.

MRS DE A. I assumed that the assessors would use a tape-measure. But no, can you imagine, they did it by triangulation. Fifty-three metres. By triangulation. I have the report.

DR LEBRUN. At least you have the comfort of knowing it was instantaneous.

MRS DE A. That depends whether or not you include the fall in the overall picture. I have the report. It's all in the assessor's report.

DR LEBRUN (*tentative*). And may I ask . . . What reason your husband had to be anxious?

MRS DE A. None at all, Doctor. That was his problem.

DR LEBRUN. Ah . . .

MRS DE A. Do you know whenever he was having one of his so-called bad days you would find him standing by that window counting his blessings. His blessings, yes, can you imagine? His talented daughter, his own wonderful voice, his excellent health, his cosy apartment — and of course modesty forbids me to mention myself, who stood by

him as you can imagine through thick and thin — but as you can see
the list is a long one — no end of blessings in fact. And that was his
problem you see. Because what he really wanted to do was suffer,
that was where he felt his talent lay, but what with all his blessings
he didn't know where to begin.

DR LEBRUN. Suffer?

MRS DE A. Oh not just for himself you understand, but for humanity.

Pause. Faint click of opened door.

Ah, there you are Rose. Rose, this is Doctor Lebrun. From the
Conservatory. He's come to hear you play.

DR LEBRUN. Good afternoon Rose. I'm very pleased to meet you.

MRS DE A. Curtsey to the doctor, Rose.

DR LEBRUN. Your mother's been telling me all about you.

MRS DE A. Hardly all, Doctor. Curtsey to the doctor, Rose. (*Sotto
voce:*) I forgot to mention, Rose ceased verbal expression immediately
after the incident I have described. She has not yet resumed. I meant
to say. (*Aloud:*) That's it, Rose. Do a nice curtsey.

DR LEBRUN (*sotto voce*). Is it serious?

MRS DE A (*sotto voce*). It's just one of her moods I'm sure. She has
these moods. It doesn't affect her playing in the least. (*Aloud:*) Your
frock looks very pretty, Rose. Don't you think her frock looks
pretty, Doctor?

DR LEBRUN (*Aloud*). It's certainly very fetching.

MRS DE A. Did you hear that, Rose. Doctor Lebrun says he's quite
stunned by it. I ran it up myself you know, on the Singer. No pattern
of course. Completely out of my own head.

DR LEBRUN. I'd never have guessed, Mrs de A.

MRS DE A. You don't think it's too grown-up for her, do you?

Silence.

I wanted it to be striking of course but on the other hand I'm sure
you'll agree there's nothing worse than an overdressed child.

DR LEBRUN. It would not look out of place on the concert platform,
Mrs de A. A soloist, particularly a lady soloist, is quite entitled, if not
indeed expected, to take certain . . . liberties.

MRS DE A. I agonised over the feathers. Rose . . . Don't! I'm sorry,
Doctor, but I can't make her stop biting her nails. Stop it, Rose. Her
father was the same. Sometimes she bleeds you know, over the keys.
Stop it, Rose, or you'll bleed again. You know sometimes I think she
wants to make herself bleed, just to worry me.

DR LEBRUN. It will pass, Mrs de A. Peversity does not last.

MRS DE A. I'm dreading puberty, Doctor, simply dreading it.

DR LEBRUN. Puberty? (*Slight pause.*) I must admit . . . I was under the impression . . .

MRS DE A. It's the frock, Doctor. And her bones. She has large bones for her age. But mainly the frock. When she sits at the stool like that you see it puffs out around her hips, but it's all material of course, all material, she's got no hips to speak of, nothing of that sort at all. No, puberty's some way off I think you'll find, some considerable way off. I'm sure we're both better off without it for the time being.

A single sustained note sounds in the middle register of the piano.

DR LEBRUN. We're neglecting our pianist, Mrs de A.

The note continues to sound, then stops.

What is she going to play for us?

MRS DE A. I think she's going to do the Mozart. Isn't that right, Rose? The Mozart? Yes, she'll begin with the Mozart, Doctor. The Mozart has always been her favourite.

A pause. Then ROSE *plays without repeats, the first eighteen bars — the entire theme — of Mozart's Piano Sonata in A, (K331), on a well-tuned good quality piano. Her performance starts well enough, but after the first two bars her playing becomes characterised by occasional wrong notes, always rapidly corrected, repetition of some short phrases, and eccentric fluctuations of tempo, for example sudden hurrying on the two occasions when the opening bars recur. The impression in other words is of an ill-taught novice. As soon as the final chord is released,* MRS DE A *begins to clap vigorously*

(*Clapping.*) Bravo, Rose! It was wonderful. Now stand up. That's it, stand up. Curtsey to the doctor. That's right. And another. That's lovely.

The clapping stops.

Now back to the stool, Rose. Back to the stool. (*Pause.*) I do adore that melody, don't you, Doctor? (*Slight pause.*) Oh, of course I realise that to a distinguished member of the Conservatory her performance may seem a little unrefined, and perhaps it's not quite in conformity with current public taste about which I'm sure you'll agree the least said the better. But the crucial thing, don't you think, is her depth, her depth of feeling, and her range, her emotional range. That's why she goes her own way at times with the music. She feels it that way. Don't you, Rose? She's not just a machine like some of these so-called pianists on the radio who obviously just want to get to the end of their piece in the shortest possible time. She's not afraid to linger. She's not afraid of an emotional interpretation. That's what sets her apart, don't you think?

Pause.

DR LEBRUN. Perhaps I could hear a little more . . . before . . . forming an opinion, Mrs de A.

MRS DE A. But of course! Rose would be delighted. Wouldn't you, Rose? The doctor would like an encore. Play him your Bach.

DR LEBRUN. Perhaps she would like to go on to the first variation. Could you play me the first variation please, Rose?

MRS DE A. She does the Bach wonderfully.

DR LEBRUN. I would be interested to hear the first variation.

MRS DE A. Do you know the First Variation, Rose?

DR LEBRUN. I'm sure she must, Mrs de A.

MRS DE A. I don't think she does. Do you know the First Variation, Rose? It seems the doctor's rather fond of it. Is it in your green book? Who is it by, Doctor? We can look in the index.

DR LEBRUN. Mozart, Mrs de A. It's by Mozart.

MRS DE A. Ah! Of course! Mozart's First Variation. Look in the index, Rose. It's at the front.

DR LEBRUN. I think you will find it follows the theme which she has just played.

MRS DE A. Surely not, Doctor. The index is at the front.

DR LEBRUN. Not the index, Mrs de A. The first variation. The first variation will follow the theme which she has just played. There is no other place for it.

MRS DE A. With respect, Doctor, the Bach is next. Page 10, the Mozart. Page 11, the Bach. I'm quite sure of that. I know those pieces like the back of my hand. Look in the index, Rose.

DR LEBRUN. It really doesn't matter, Mrs de A.

MRS DE A. Under M, Rose. M for mother.

DR LEBRUN. It's really not important, Mrs de A. Let her play the Bach instead.

MRS DE A. Try the red book, Rose.

DR LEBRUN. The Bach will do very nicely.

MRS DE A. I thought you wanted Mozart's First Variation, Doctor Lebrun.

DR LEBRUN. I'd be quite happy with the Bach.

MRS DE A. With respect, Doctor, you led us to believe when we first offered you the Bach that you would find nothing more abhorrent, that nothing but this esoteric First Variation of yours would do.

DR LEBRUN. That wasn't my intention, Mrs de A.

MRS DE A. With respect, Doctor, Rose and I can't be expected to divine

your intentions. We can only listen to what you say, and trust that
you mean it. It is particularly distressing for Rose to have her
programme chopped and changed about like this. You can see the
state she's in.

DR LEBRUN. I meant no harm, Mrs de A.

MRS DE A. For all we know this piece of yours may not even be
available from our shop. Heaven knows it's hard enough to get that
Mr Cook to stock the classics as it is, without pestering him with
special requests. (*Pause.*) Play the Bach, Rose. (*Slight pause.*) Page 11.
(*Slight pause.*) Green book.

A short silence, then ROSE *begins to play Bach's Prelude in C Major,
Number 1 of the First Book of the Well-tempered Klavier. There are
no wrong notes this time, but the flowing arpeggio figure is heavy and
uneven. Uncertainty is apparent at each bar's change of harmony.*

(*At about bar 3, sotto voce:*) I do adore the harmonies, don't you?

The music continues.

(*Sotto voce:*) Do you hear how she brings them out?

The music continues.
*At about bar 5 a dull knocking sound can be heard. The music
continues. The knocking becomes more vigorous.*

Louder, Rose.

The music continues. The knocking persists.

DR LEBRUN. What is that, Mrs de A?

MRS DE A. A vampire, Doctor. Take no notice. He has no soul. Louder,
Rose.

The music continues, louder. The knocking persists.

The man says he works at night would you believe, and sleeps during
the day. In a coffin I shouldn't wonder. Since don't you agree, if he
were human the music would surely soothe him. Heaven alone knows
what all that banging must do to the ceiling of his apartment.

(*She shouts:*) Vampire!

The music falters.

Don't stop, Rose.

The music recovers.

Don't give in to him. What that man needs, Doctor, is a stake, a stake
through the heart.

The music falters. The knocking persists.

Don't stop, Rose. Don't stop.

The music recovers.

I've tried to reason with him, but he won't answer the door. (*She shouts:*) Why can't you leave us in peace!

The music stops.

Don't stop, Rose. It's very unprofessional to stop. Isn't it, Doctor? She shouldn't stop under any circumstances, should she?

The knocking has also stopped.

I've always taught her never to stop. It's just not done. On the radio they never stop. Only at the end. For the announcements. Not half way through. It's just not done. She should play until she drops if need be, shouldn't she? Go on, Rose. Take no notice of that Philistine. Carry on.

Silence.

Carry on, Rose.

Silence.

(*Violently, between clenched teeth:*) Rose! Finish your piece!

Silence.

DR LEBRUN. I think it is quite understandable, Mrs de A, and perfectly in keeping with one's professional obligations, that Rose should not wish to continue, under the circumstances. (*Gently:*) Thank you for playing to us, Rose. It has been most enjoyable.

MRS DE A. With respect, Doctor, I don't think it helps matters to make allowances on her behalf. She really ought to finish her piece. It's not like her not to finish a piece of music once she's started. She's usually so determined to reach the end.

Rose! Stop that! Do you want to cripple yourself? Do you?

She's usually such a determined girl.

You may think it's fun to bloody the keys in your own home, but I can tell you they'll take a very dim view of that sort of thing in the Conservatory. Isn't that so, Doctor? You won't be able to rely on the doctor here always putting in a good word for you. He'll have his other students to think of too. Won't you, Doctor? (*Pause.*)

You know I really don't understand it. She's never not finished a piece before. She's usually so determined as I say to reach the end. She takes after Mr de A in that respect. He was a determined man, a terribly determined man. (*Pause.*)

He wanted to suffer he did I say. That was where he felt his talent lay. That was where he felt he could have made his mark. (*Pause.*)

You know it was his third attempt? The time before the porter discovered him on top of the lift. He'd thrown himself down the shaft you see, but evidently he hadn't realised the lift was just a few floors below. Normally you see it's stuck at the top of the building. He sprained every muscle in his neck. It ruined his voice, ruined it.

But after that I could see he meant business. Charlie, I used to say, Charlie, I realise now that you are determined either to do away with yourself or die in the attempt. (*Brief laugh.*) His sense of humour was quite unimpaired, you see.

Silence.

Come along, Rose. Finish your piece.

Silence.

It's just not the same without the end.

Silence.

Please, Rose. Finish it for us.

A pause, then ROSE *begins to play the Bach Prelude again. She begins at bar 24 and goes through to the end. She plays as before, that is with no wrong notes, but inaccurately in other ways. As she nears the end of the piece, however, there is a new sense of energy and momentum in her playing, and the final three bars are at the same time strident and triumphant.*

PLOUGHBOY MONDAY

by David Pownall

For Uncle Fred and Auntie Marjorie

David Pownall was born in Liverpool in 1938. He was educated at Lord
Wandsworth College and the University of Keele. After graduating, he
worked in the British Motor industry and Zambian copper mining for
ten years. In 1969 he returned to England and, after two years with
Century Theatre, on tour in the north-west, he became a full-time
novelist and playwright. In 1975 he founded the new-play touring
company, Paines Plough, with John Adams. Between 1972 and 1976
he was resident playwright at the Duke's Playhouse, Lancaster. His stage
plays, which have been performed nationally and internationally, include
Music to Murder By, *Motocar*, *Richard III Part 2*, *Barricade*, *An
Audience Called Edouard*, *Livingstone and Sechele*, *Masterclass*, *The
Viewing*, and an adaptation of *Pride and Prejudice*.

His most recent television play is *The First Ascent of Mont Blanc* (BBC).
He has five published novels, *The Raining Tree War* and *African Horse*
(for which he was made a Fellow of the Royal Society of Literature,
God Perkins, *Light on the Honeycomb* and *Beloved Latitudes*, as well
as collections of short stories. His many radio plays include *Beef*, winner
of a Giles Cooper Award in 1981, and also a John Whiting award.

Ploughboy Monday was first broadcast on BBC Radio 4 on 9 November 1985. The cast was as follows:

HAROLD	Jason Littler
VERA } MAUD }	Judith Barker
GEORGE	Geoffrey Hinsliff
GRUNNIDGE	Geoffrey Banks
STAN	Colin Meredith
PERKINS	Gabriel Paul Gawin
VALERIE } ROSE }	Lesley Nicol
HAYWOOD } RICE }	Malcolm Hebden
COOK GLADYS } TILLY }	Ruth Holden
YATES } FARMER }	James Tomlinson
MATCH JUDGE MEGAPHONE VOICE }	Randal Herley
BROUGH MANLEY } OWNER }	Paul Webster

Director: Alfred Bradley
Running time, as broadcast: 70 minutes 21 seconds.

The parlour of the Ransom home. In the background, popular early twenties music is crackling. VERA *has been talking for several minutes before we hear her.* GEORGE, *her husband, is in the room.*

VERA. It doesn't make any sense to me at all. What's light work? Doing the weighbridge? I could manage that. (*Pause.*) When you come home and go off doing gardening jobs you dig, don't you? That's not light work — digging. You want to talk to the under manager about getting taken off light work. And what happens if you get a bad back doing gardening? You won't get compensation, you know, not for casual work. There's never any overtime on the weighbridge, is there? (*Pause.*) You should show them that you can manage proper work. I know you don't like asking but we need the money. (*Pause.*) You could ask.

GEORGE. The doctor lays down what I can do. Nothing can move him. And keep your mouth shut about gardening.

HAROLD. Mum, I'm home.

VERA. There's a pie out for you and some pickles.

HAROLD. Did timbering this evening, Dad. Stresses and strains.

VERA. Who taught you tonight, Harold? Anyone we know?

HAROLD. No, he was from Warsop Main. Good though. He knows Alan Brough . . .

VERA. *Mr* Brough. If he's to be your deputy down the pit, Harold, you must treat him with proper respect.

HAROLD. He doesn't mind.

VERA. Well, he should. I've never heard of any deputy allowing an apprentice to call him by his Christian name. It's not right.

HAROLD. Yes, Mum.

VERA. Your father would never think of calling Mr Brough anything but Mr Brough.

HAROLD. No, Mum.

VERA. Eat your supper.

HAROLD. Is this a pie I made?

He sits down at the table.

VERA. I don't put labels on them, Harold.

HAROLD. But it could be?

VERA. Get on with it. You have to be up early for school.

HAROLD. Your pies are famous, Mum. That's how people know me. I'm the son of the woman who makes Mrs Ransom's pies, they say. She makes marvellous pies.

GEORGE. She's the cat's mother. And don't call your mother a woman.

VERA. He's only repeating what he's heard folk say.

HAROLD. Sorry, Mum. Can I grind the meat up tomorrow?

VERA. If you behave yourself. Now be quiet. Your father wants to listen to the news.

Radio news from June 1930 that will identify the period — industrial news of a general nature to do with the slump would fit. It fades. The parlour atmosphere fades.

The kitchen of the Ransom home. The clattering of trays as VERA *bakes pies. It is 5.30 in the morning, August 1930. Birdsong can be heard through open windows.*

HAROLD. Thirty-four, thirty-five, thirty-six, thirty-seven, thirty-eight . . . any more I haven't seen, Mum?

VERA. Did you count the batch in the oven?

HAROLD. I think so. They were the first I counted. It must be thirty-eight . . .

VERA. Must be isn't *is*, is it? I must know exactly. Count them again and concentrate, Harold. I've got customers . . .

There is a knock on the door of the back kitchen.

HAROLD. How many's in the oven?

The door opens.

VERA. A dozen. Good morning.

HAROLD. That's twelve, thirteen, fourteen . . .

He counts on behind the dialogue.

HAYWOOD. Morning, Mrs Ransom. Two pies, love — one hot, one cold.

VERA. That's tenpence, Mr Haywood.

HAYWOOD. Hello, young Harold. When d'you start work down t'pit?

HAROLD. Twenty-three . . . twenty-three . . . oh, don't let me forget the number . . . twenty-three . . . it's today, Mr Haywood. I'm off in a minute.

HAYWOOD. Are you walking in with your dad? You'll be able to go together.

HAROLD. Oh, hell. I'm lost now. I can't remember those I've counted and those I haven't. Yes, Mr Haywood. I'll be going in with my dad. I'm starting today with Mr Brough. He's my deputy.

HAYWOOD. He's all right is Brough. Work hard, young Harold. Make your mum and dad proud of you. Ta-ra.

The door closes.

HAROLD. I'm going to be late if I don't watch it. Where's me dad?

VERA. He's gone in early.

HAROLD. Oh. D'you mind if I go now, Mum? I still think it's thirty-eight, but only think.

VERA. Go on then. There's your break. You don't have to guess what it is.

HAROLD. Thanks, Mum. Wish me luck.

VERA. It's not luck you'll need down the mine, Harold. Stay away from bad types and troublemakers. Do your job as you're told to do it. No answering back.

HAROLD. Yes, Mum. Can I go now?

VERA. You can't wait, can you? Your first day at work and you can't wait.

HAROLD. No, I can't. I've been dreaming about this, Mum. I've got a mining job. It's a job for life, they say. That's how I want it. I'll come straight home and tell you all about it. Bye, Mum.

The door opens and HAROLD *runs in his boots down a side entrance. A pause filled with birdsong. The door closes.*

VERA. Twelve in there . . . thirteen, fourteen, fifteen, sixteen . . .

Her voice fades.

The cap-lamp room.
The sound of lamp batteries being put down on the counter, boots, the hum of talk.
BROUGH's *voice fades in.*

BROUGH. . . . while the cap-lamp is in your possession, Harold, it's your responsibility. I don't want to find you playing games with it, swinging it round your head, knocking it about. Any damage you'll pay for, understand?

HAROLD. Yes, Mr Brough.

BROUGH. When you get your cap-lamp you tie the belt and battery round your waist like this . . . see, make it firm, and run the cable up your back and over your left shoulder if you're right-handed or your right shoulder if you're left-handed. It keeps it out of the road while you're working.

HAROLD. Yes, Mr Brough. I remember. We did it at night school.

BROUGH. Give this lad a lamp in there.

GEORGE. He'll get no lamp here.

BROUGH. George . . . what are you doing in the cap lamp room? I thought you were on the weighbridge.

GEORGE. No son of mine is going down the pit.

HAROLD. Oh, Dad . . . no . . .

BROUGH. God, George, the lad's been going to night classes for three years. He's got his certificate . . . the lad's done well!

GEORGE. I've been in three rock falls. I'm a cripple, fit for nothing. The only job they'll give me is charity. My son isn't going to end up like that.

HAROLD. I want to be a miner, like you. What's the matter with that?

BROUGH. You could have spoken up before now. We'll all look fools, you most of all.

GEORGE. That doesn't worry me none. Go home, Harold. There's nothing for you here. It's my right as your father to stop you if I want.

HAROLD. Dad, please! I've got me heart set on it . . .

GEORGE. Go home and do as you're told. I'll talk to you tonight.

HAROLD. Talk to me? You've never talked to me! You've never talked to anyone but yourself!

HAROLD runs out.
Some laughter from the other miners in the queue.

BROUGH. You've done a lot of damage there, George. But then, you'll have thought of that, won't you? Get back on the weighbridge and keep out of my way for a few weeks.

GEORGE. He never asked my permission. You never asked my permission. My own bloody wife never asked my permission. I was taken for granted and see where it's got you.

BROUGH. You stupid, stupid man. God help you.

The sounds of cap-lamp room fade.

The parlour of the Ransom home. The only sound is the ticking of the clock.
The back door opens and closes.
Heavy boots come close, very slow. GEORGE *sits down. The ticking of the clock gets louder.*

GEORGE. Take my boots off for me.

VERA. That's a job I'll never do for you again.

GEORGE. Tell Harold I want to speak to him.

VERA. He's gone.

GEORGE. Where to?

VERA. I don't know.

GEORGE. Pie for tea, I suppose. That's taken for granted. (*Pause.*) It's for his own good.

The radio is on: dance music.

VERA. You've taken his only chance away. There's no other work in this place. My only child and you've driven him out of his own home. I know him, George. He's like you. He won't forgive. We've lost him. That's all there is to it.

GEORGE. He'll be back. He can help you with the pies. He likes playing with pastry, it strikes me. But the pit's not pastry. The pit's only pain.

The parlour atmosphere fades, with the ticking of the clock being asserted over the music.

HAROLD (*in his head*). Bloody old bastard doing that to me in front of everyone, leading me on deliberately, never saying a word. I'd never end up like him anyway. He's always been half-asleep, bloody accident-prone old sod . . . God, I hate him, I hate him . . .

The open road on a summer evening, birdsong, cattle being driven.

STAN. Hey up, watch yourself. You'll get trod on.

HAROLD. Where is this?

STAN. Laxton Common. I don't know your face. What are you doing round here?

HAROLD. Just out walking.

STAN. Late to be out walking.

HAROLD. I just kept going until I was lost. Didn't think about it.

STAN. Where are you going to sleep?

HAROLD. Oh, I don't know. Up a tree.

STAN. Why don't you go home?

HAROLD. I've left home.

STAN. Go back then. Or have they sold your bed?

HAROLD. I'll never go back — well, not for a long time. Not till I've shown him.

STAN. Oh, you're showing someone, are you?

HAROLD. Fallen out with me dad. He's a right old bugger.

STAN. Mine's a right old bugger an' all. But I've given up showing him. He never takes a blind bit of notice.

HAROLD. Got anything to eat?

STAN. No. Come up to the farm and I'll get you something. You can doss in the barn if you like.

HAROLD. Won't they mind?

STAN. Mind? They won't even see you. The farm is so big they don't know what they've got on it.

HAROLD. What's the money like?

STAN. Thirteen pounds a year with food and lodging — that's boy's rate. I was on that last year. It's not much but it's better than nowt.

Fade on cattle being driven and a dog barking.

The foreman's office at the farm.

GRUNNIDGE. If you're from a pit village, son, why aren't you going down the pit? It's what you'd get used to. Farming is different from mining. Not the same thing at all.

HAROLD. Never fancied going down the pit, sir. I like the open air.

GRUNNIDGE. What does your father think?

HAROLD. He's dead, sir.

GRUNNIDGE. How old are you?

HAROLD. Fourteen. I know I'm small, but I'm fourteen. Honestly, sir, I can prove it.

GRUNNIDGE. I think you better had. We'll write to your mother.

HAROLD. That's fine, sir. She'll have my birth certificate.

GRUNNIDGE. You're lucky, turning up on the doorstep like this. The boy has gone down with meningitis and his family say it's working up here that's done it. You were in the right place at the right time. I should cultivate that if you want to get along with me. I can't stand latecomers or shirkers. You're an opportunist. You'll find it very useful up here. Know your place, do your work, and you'll get on. You can start tomorrow.

HAROLD. Thanks for giving me a chance, sir. I'll work hard and I won't let you down, I promise.

GRUNNIDGE. Don't stick your neck out. Now bugger off. I'm busy.

Fade.

The farm dormitory.

HAROLD. They say you're Mr Perkins. I have to see you.

PERKINS. Are you Tommy's replacement?

HAROLD. Was Tommy the one with meningitis?

PERKINS. Aye. He said it was the wind always whistling in his ears that did it. I'm the fourth waggoner. All right. There's the third waggoner, the second waggoner and the first waggoner, he's *the* waggoner in charge.

HAROLD. Where do I sleep?

PERKINS. In here.

HAROLD. Do you always lie on other people's beds with your boots on?

PERKINS. It's my bed as well.

HAROLD. But I've always had my own bed.

PERKINS. Well, you'll have to get used to sharing. Once you get in, don't move, don't wriggle, don't snore and don't fart and we'll get on. With Tommy I said he could read for twenty minutes, or talk, once he was in bed — if I felt like talking. Remember, I'd like my own bed as well. And I'm the boss, here, and outside. You look up to me.

HAROLD. Who says?

PERKINS. I have to take care of you. There's some funny customers amongst the cowmen, the shepherds and the labourers, but you'll find the waggoners are mostly all right. But keep your eye open.

Fade.

The sound of the waggoners fast asleep.
HAROLD *is crying softly.*

PERKINS. There's nothing to worry about, Harold. Have a good cry tonight and get up in the morning having cleared your mind. This is your home now and you do things our way.

Fade.

Fade in the stable and PERKINS.

PERKINS. You'll be on boy's jobs, locking up the chickens, helping with the milking, mucking out, thistle-spudding, anything that's got no skill.

One day they could put you on the plough. We plough all year on this farm. Never stop. There're eighteen horses. We look after them as well as ourselves. What do you know about horses?

HAROLD. Nothing.

PERKINS. Everybody knows something about horses.

HAROLD. I mean nothing useful.

PERKINS. Horses have power and strength, but they're a bit thick, like some people. I'm going to be head waggoner before I've finished and I'll do it through knowing horses. There's no other way. D'you want to learn?

HAROLD. Yes, I do. I have to.

PERKINS. Plenty don't these days. We only have three kinds of horses here — Shires, Suffolks and one hunter for the trap and riding. Show me an entire in this lot.

HAROLD. An entire what?

PERKINS. An entire horse, stupid.

HAROLD. They're all entire horses as far as I can see.

PERKINS. That's where you're wrong, Harold mate. An entire is a stallion that's entire, not a gelding, a complete horse. All right? It's a new language you're having to learn so think on — keep your ears pricked — and remember, even carting muck has a craft to it.

HAROLD. Same as mining is then. They even taught us how to use a shovel at night school.

PERKINS. You went to night school for mining? What the hell are you doing here then?

HAROLD. I changed me mind. Let's say I didn't like the idea of being in the dark.

Fade.

An open field. The sound of ploughing with three horses. Gulls.

PERKINS. Bodkin. We're ploughing bodkin, Harold.

HAROLD. Right. Bodkin.

PERKINS. Ploughing with three horses, two in the furrow and one on the land is bodkin. What type of ground are we ploughing, Harold?

HAROLD. Clay.

PERKINS. Strong clay. Why are we ploughing it?

HAROLD. Break it up, kill the weeds, aerate the soil, prepare . . .

PERKINS. Show me the cross-aim. (*Pause.*) Show me the swindle-trees. (*Pause.*) Take the ayles.

HAROLD. What's the ayles?

PERKINS. The handles, stupid. Come on. Have a try.

HAROLD. I won't get it right . . . hey, it's not such a strain, is it?

PERKINS. The two horses on the land are pulling sideways, you have to
counter that. My ploughing's not so good today. Over my shoulder
I'm aware of running out, dog's hind-legs and pencil-lines on my
seams. Don't be confused. Setting your rig is everything, Harold.
I didn't set my share at the proper distance from my coulter and my
wadsticks are all over the place. Drinking, Harold, beware of drinking.
Doesn't go with ploughing. This field has had sheep on it so I
shouldn't be ploughing deeper than one and a half inches. One and a
half inches for sheep, Harold. Keep the dung in the top level. Better
than night school, eh?

HAROLD. You're a torment, Mr Perkins.

PERKINS. I love to see a lad learning something.

Fade.

The foreman's office.

GRUNNIDGE. You'd better sit down, young man.

HAROLD. What is it, Mr Grunnidge?

GRUNNIDGE. I wrote to your mother, as I said I had to. That was two
months ago and I hadn't had a reply so I did some checking up
through a friend. Did you know that your mum and dad weren't in
that house any more?

HAROLD. Not in our house? Who says they're not?

GRUNNIDGE. Someone went round. There's a different family
altogether living there now. Nobody ever mentioned to you that
they might be moving away?

HAROLD. No.

GRUNNIDGE. So you don't know where they are?

HAROLD. No.

GRUNNIDGE. But you do know that your dad's not dead like you told
me he was. (*Pause.*) Why did you tell me a lie like that?

HAROLD. I'm sorry.

GRUNNIDGE. Puts me in a spot. It's nothing to do with me if you don't
get on with your family, is it? But we'll have to find them, or you'll
have to.

HAROLD. Yes, Mr Grunnidge.

GRUNNIDGE. Of course, it might take a while. There's a lot of ploughing work. Can't spare anyone. You'll have to wait until next May before you get a break. When's your birthday?

HAROLD. December. But I'm already fourteen, like I said.

GRUNNIDGE. Well, maybe. Don't you need your mother though? I thought every lad needed his mother.

HAROLD. I'll catch up with her one day.

GRUNNIDGE. Well, only you will know if that's enough. We're pleased with you, Harold. Work first, worries second. Go on, hop it.

HAROLD. Thank you, Mr Grunnidge.

Fade.

The dormitory.
The sounds of men and boys asleep and HAROLD *whimpering.*

PERKINS (*whispering*). Come on, Harold. Cut that out. Everyone can hear you. (*Pause.*) What's up?

HAROLD. Nothing.

PERKINS. Nobody cries about nothing. What did Grunnidge want?

HAROLD. To say I'm doing all right.

PERKINS. That's enough to make anyone cry, I suppose. Hey, tell us what's up or stop snivelling. (*Pause.*) I'm supposed to help you, you know. I can't if you don't tell me anything.

HAROLD. I don't have a home any more. Me mum and dad have left our house. I don't know where they've gone.

PERKINS. They'll turn up one day. Think on the bright side, Harold. If you haven't got a home you can't be homesick. A man's job is his home, anyway.

HAROLD. They don't care about me.

PERKINS. They don't have to. You're supposed to be taking care of yourself.

HAROLD. That doesn't mean they should just forget about me.

PERKINS. Maybe they just got fed up living there.

HAROLD. No, they liked it. They've moved away so I can't find them. And I won't. I won't even look. They can rot for all I care. (*Pause.*) Well, me dad can rot. Me mum's all right.

PERKINS. It's all right you saying that. Both my parents are dead. I miss having someone. In fact I think you shouldn't say things like that about your father, no matter how hard he is. It's bad luck apart from anything else.

HAROLD. I can't help it, Mr Perkins.

PERKINS. You can call me Joe from now on.

HAROLD. Thanks, Joe.

PERKINS. You can look on me like a father if you like.

HAROLD. But you're only nineteen . . . Joe.

PERKINS. It's old enough to be your father.

Fade.

An open field. The sound of four horses harrowing.

PERKINS. Harrowing this clay after the frost has been at it is like crumbling sugar. It's the easiest job you'll get.

HAROLD. Except for shutting up the chickens. I can't stand doing that. It makes me feel like no one at all.

PERKINS. I had to do it. It's a farm boy's job.

HAROLD. If Grunnidge wants the chickens shut up he should do it himself.

PERKINS. I can see that happening. After thirty years in farming he'll want to spend his time chasing hens around a field.

HAROLD. It's not a job at all. They should train a dog to do it. They herd up sheep and cows, why not chickens?

PERKINS. You want to tell that idea to Grunnidge. He'd like to hear it. Chickens can't abide dogs, Harold. To them there's no difference between a farm dog and a fox. And a chicken is always in a panic. It doesn't trust anyone.

HAROLD. It's about time I got some proper jobs to do, that's all.

PERKINS. You've only been here five minutes.

The sound of an approaching lorry.

HAROLD. If Grunnidge tells me to lock up the chickens tonight, I'm going to say no.

PERKINS. Let me be around when you do it. I don't think he knows that he's got such a Bolshie on the property.

The lorry stops close by.

Here's your chance. Go on, tell old Grunnidge he can chase his own chickens. I want to hear you.

GRUNNIDGE. Harold! Come over here.

PERKINS. Hope it's not trouble you're in.

HAROLD. Shouldn't be. I haven't done anything wrong.

GRUNNIDGE. Hurry up, I haven't got all day.

HAROLD *runs over to* GRUNNIDGE. *Away from the harrow that keeps moving.*

HAROLD (*fade in*). What is it, Mr Grunnidge?

GRUNNIDGE. Get in the lorry.

The sounds of the open fields fade.

Fade in the lorry cab atmosphere and its noise as it drives off.

HAROLD. Where are we going?

GRUNNIDGE. We have to pick up something near your home. I thought you could go along and see what you can find out about your parents.

HAROLD. What, like this? I don't want to go back all dirty . . .

GRUNNIDGE. I brought your clean clothes. They're under the seat.

HAROLD. But I don't need to find out . . .

GRUNNIDGE. You're a cold-hearted little tyke. If you don't go and find out, I will. By heck, they must have done something to upset you. What was it? Did they cut off your toffee ration?

HAROLD. I've left home. I'm taking care of mysen now . . .

GRUNNIDGE. And they don't matter anymore? They bring you up, feed you, clothe you, protect you — and then it means nothing. I wouldn't like a son like that.

HAROLD. There's plenty of time for me to find them later on.

GRUNNIDGE. If you know what's happening. And you don't.

Fade.

Fade in the exterior of the Ransom house.
A knock on the door. It is opened.

YATES. What d'you want?

HAROLD. I used to live here.

YATES. Well, you don't live here now.

HAROLD. My mum and dad lived here last.

YATES. Was the name Ransom?

HAROLD. That's right.

YATES. So, you're one of them Ransoms, are you? You didn't take care of this house much.

HAROLD. Yes, we did. It was always kept spotless.

YATES. Threw you out, did they? Or have you been to Borstal?

HAROLD. I'm working. The post hasn't been arriving . . . I just wondered if they'd left an address . . .

YATES. No, they haven't.

HAROLD. Oh.

YATES. There's been a few people looking for your parents.

HAROLD. It's a mix-up of some sort.

YATES. That's what I thought. What were they running away from? You?

HAROLD. It had nothing to do with me. I'm working now.

YATES. You don't know anything about them moving?

HAROLD. As I said, I've been working . . . far away. (*Pause.*) You haven't heard anything?

YATES. Your dad left the mine so he had to leave the house. Somebody said he'd taken up gardening, working on an estate somewhere. Where your mother went, I don't know.

HAROLD. She'll have gone with him.

YATES. Oh, no. She left before that.

HAROLD. Where did she go?

YATES. Your dad didn't even know that. (*Pause.*) Someone should at least have told you that. I heard she'd done a bunk.

HAROLD. She'll have gone to stay at my gran's . . . both of them will have.

YATES. That's what's happened. Perhaps your gran's been poorly. Now, I'm in the middle of me tea . . . I'll have to close the door.

HAROLD. If you hear anything, will you write to me?

YATES. Yes, yes. I'll keep you up to date.

HAROLD. I'll send you the address.

YATES. All right. Good luck. Off you go.

The door closes.

HAROLD (*in his head*). I can't remember me granny's address . . . would I ever find it? I'll ask Mum's friends . . .

TILLY. No, Harold, she just went, overnight. No with or by your leave . . .

ROSE. Well, you know your father, Harold, after your mum had gone he said even less than he usually did, which was never much. Then he packed up and left. Didn't say goodbye to anyone . . .

MAUD. My own opinion, Harold, is that she left because of you. It just wasn't worth her living with him after you'd gone . . .

GLADYS. She said to me once — he's flown the nest, and the nest is no longer any use to me.

HAROLD (*in his head*). Mum! Where are you?

Fade in the lorry cab.

GRUNNIDGE. So, how d'you get on, Harold?

HAROLD. Me mum's gone to me granny's near Rotherham. Me dad's doing gardening work and looking for a house.

GRUNNIDGE. Oh, plenty of information then.

HAROLD. I asked the neighbours.

GRUNNIDGE. I'll be able to write to your mum . . . at your granny's then.

HAROLD. Yes. I'll get the address.

GRUNNIDGE. Ah. You haven't got it on you?

HAROLD. I'll have it somewhere. What have we got in the back?

GRUNNIDGE. Seed-corn, Harold. For planting, you know.

  The lorry cab fades.

Fade in the open field. The sound of ploughing in the rain. Fade in
PERKINS.

PERKINS. Oh, God, I'll be glad when this's finished. The horses are paddling in mud. Run up and bring the new horse round, Harold.

HAROLD. Gee again, come on . . . gee again.

PERKINS. Gee again, you great idiot! God, he's a numbskull this one.

HAROLD. Stupid lump! You'd think he'd have learnt by now.

  Sounds of the turning plough.
  Thunder.
  The horses crash and shake in the traces.

PERKINS. Hold his head! Hold his head! Grab hold of his ears if you can!

HAROLD. I've got him. Stand still you gormless thing. It's only thunder . . . (*More soothing.*) Only thunder . . . you'll be all right . . . there we are.

PERKINS. Hold him until the storm passes. I don't think we can do much more on this. The mud's just getting thicker and thicker.

  More thunder.

HAROLD. Steady now. Nothing will hurt thee . . . we'll go home soon . . . get in the dry and I'll rub you down . . .

PERKINS. Grunnidge says your parents are in Rotherham.

HAROLD. He should mind his own business for a change.

PERKINS. Oh, I shouldn't say that. He's taken a shine to you.

HAROLD. Gently now. He's trembling all over . . . there, you're safe
with me . . .

PERKINS. Gardening, he said. That's the same line as you, really. You're
in gardening on a big scale. Farming's gardening, isn't it?

HAROLD. How long are we going to stand out here in this rain?

PERKINS. It'll pass. There's no point in us arriving back before time
with the sun starting to shine. We'll wait.

A tremendous clap of thunder.
The horses lunge in the traces.
The plough is pulled over.

Don't let go of that horse's head, Harold! Christ, that was close.
Did you feel it? Bloody lightning nearly hit the plough.

Fade.

Fade in a large horse team with a roller moving quickly, and PERKINS.

PERKINS. Four horses in hand now, Harold. In Canada they have
twenty and they plough for twenty-four hours in one line, then turn
and plough twenty-four hours in the opposite direction. So don't
feel hard done by. At least you don't have to sleep out.

HAROLD. They can get up a fair speed, can't they?

PERKINS. With the Cambridge roller they can. It's only a big wheel,
after all. We're bloody charioteers, Romans!

HAROLD. Ploughing is plodding . . . I like plodding.

PERKINS. And paddling. You can race with the roller. Giddiup!

The roller goes faster.
The sound of PERKINS *laughing.*

Move, you great lumps. Shift yourselves! Tanks going into battle.
Charge!

Fade.

Fade in the open field.
Ploughing sounds with two horses working.
Birdsong.

PERKINS. Gee again! Bring 'em round. Lovely. Lovely. Loveleeeee.

HAROLD. They really know what they're doing these two. They just
do it without being asked.

PERKINS. They know when it's time for a break, when it's time to go home. They know when you like them and when you don't like them.

HAROLD. Not a bad job, ploughing.

PERKINS. On a day like this, it's not. Try it in January with an east wind and you'll think different.

HAROLD. But they do it all, don't they? The horses do all the work.

PERKINS. You have to guide them. They have to do what you want them to do.

HAROLD. Would they work for me?

PERKINS. If they trusted you.

HAROLD. How would they know that?

PERKINS. They have a knack of telling.

HAROLD. They can trust me. I'll get that through to them. It's not like working, is it — being with horses — these horses. The only horses I had anything to do with were those down the pit. They had hooves covered with green slime and they brought them out once a year. My dad took me to see them come out. When they let them loose in the field these big horses rolled on their backs and kicked their legs in the air like babies. Next week they went back down again for another year.

PERKINS. That's cruel. Mining's cruel.

HAROLD (*in his head*). Not a word. Two horses side by side and not a word to each other. They just . . . do it. Do it. Do it. That's how I'd like to be. Just do it, and be done.

Fade.

Fade in the stable, and GRUNNIDGE.

GRUNNIDGE. I'm going to try you on your own. Choose your team.

HAROLD. I like this one and that one. I've come to know them.

GRUNNIDGE. That's a mare and a stallion. After April I wouldn't let you mix them. You know their names. Bonny's the mare, Fred's the . . .

HAROLD (*in his head*). I know their names. I've always known their names. Well, you two, I'm master now. You'll have to do what I say, when I say it.

GRUNNIDGE. You won't find a more docile pair of horses in all Nottinghamshire. They have natures sweeter than thine, Harold.

The sound of gulls, rooks and crows following the plough in the open field. The jangle of the plough, and labouring of two horses.

GRUNNIDGE (*fade in*). Hey, hold on, hold on . . .

HAROLD. Arve again, Dad, arve again Mum. Come round!

GRUNNIDGE (*running*). Harold, stop! What d'you think you're doing?

HAROLD. Faster! Come on Dad, lift your feet up! Mum's out-running you!

GRUNNIDGE. Harold! Stop those horses, you're driving them too hard!

HAROLD. Whoa!

The plough stops. GRUNNIDGE *and the horses are breathing hard.*

What is it, Mr Grunnidge?

GRUNNIDGE. Get off that plough.

HAROLD. I haven't finished yet.

GRUNNIDGE. You've finished all right. Listen to those horses. You're a nutcase, son. Perkins never taught you to try and plough at that speed. It's a wonder you didn't smash the rig up.

HAROLD. Well, it's light ground and it's dry, I thought I could get it done quicker and start the next field.

GRUNNIDGE. Not with two dead horses, you wouldn't. Go back to the farm and report to me after your dinner. I'll walk your horses home.

HAROLD. You'll not walk my horses home!

GRUNNIDGE. Won't I now? Don't you answer me back, lad.

HAROLD. I brought 'em out and I'll take 'em back. I'm not having everyone laughing at me.

GRUNNIDGE. You should have thought of that before you wrecked this field. It looks like I've let the pigs loose in it. Go on, get away from here before I'm tempted to belt you.

HAROLD. You raise your hand to me and I'll tell . . . I'll have the Law onto you. I know my rights . . .

GRUNNIDGE. There's a law against cruelty to animals as well, Harold. We'll have to talk about that if you're to stay on. Your job's in danger, son. Don't say anymore. Just bugger off back like I told you and we'll sort this out later. Come on Bonny, come on, Fred . . . you're all right now. Go on, you little savage! Get back to the farm!

HAROLD (*in his head*). I'll be back, Mum and Dad. Now you're lathered up I can love you. I'll plait your manes, I'll plait your tails, I'll wax your hooves and rub you down with whisky till you shine like two great big stars.

Fade in the foreman's office.

GRUNNIDGE. What's got into him, Perkins? The lad's not right.

PERKINS. I think he got carried away with himself.

GRUNNIDGE. And my horses.

PERKINS. It's his first time, Mr Grunnidge. He was on his own out there, miles away . . .

GRUNNIDGE. He was screaming at those horses, Perkins. If he'd had a whip he'd have used it. Did you tell him there's no accelerator pedal on Bonny and Fred? They have two speeds. Dead slow and stop.

PERKINS. He knows that. He knows all the horses, the time he spends in the stable.

GRUNNIDGE. There's something up with our Harold. I know what it is and I should think you do as well. But he mustn't take it out on the beasts. That's not on. I won't have it.

PERKINS. He knows that now, Mr Grunnidge. I don't think it will happen again. Things haven't been easy for him.

GRUNNIDGE. Some parents need shooting.

Fade.

Fade in the stable.

HAROLD. I have to apologise, Mum and Dad.

The sound of a restless horse.

Don't be fright. Let me come near. It will never happen again, my word on it . . . that's all over now . . .

PERKINS. Hello, Harold.

HAROLD. They don't like me now. All I get is the whites of their eyes.

PERKINS. Can't blame them, can you?

HAROLD. It was only a joke.

PERKINS. I have to go and plough that field all over again tomorrow.

A blow. The horses shy away, frightened.
HAROLD *falls.*

You've messed up my chances, Harold. Put me back a year in Grunnidge's books, you little shit! I'll beat the daylights out of you.

HAROLD. Don't fight near the horses! They'll trample me!

PERKINS. I've been working on this bloody farm for three years and things had just started to go my way when you come along and ruin everything.

A kick. The horses shy away.

HAROLD. Don't! They'll start fly-hacking!

PERKINS. I couldn't care less if they trample you to death, you stupid, selfish little sod! Who do you think you are? Something special? You're not.

HAROLD. All right, all right.

PERKINS. Come out of there. I want another swing at you.

HAROLD. You taught me, Joe. If a horse is going to start kicking, get close to it. I'm staying between these two. You're out of control.

PERKINS. Don't you come anywhere near our bed tonight. You can sleep in the midden for all I care. It's where you belong, pit-boy.

HAROLD. Better than being a bloody yokel!

PERKINS. Why don't you get back there where you belong? Go and eat bloody coal.

HAROLD. Because I can plough better than you, and I could mine better than you. I'm not thick, you see, not thick at all! (*He weeps.*)

PERKINS. I've never known such a lad for crying.

HAROLD (*furiously*). I can't help it! D'you think I want to weep in front of the likes of you?

PERKINS. You deserved it. I don't regret hitting you.

HAROLD. That didn't hurt.

PERKINS. I'll remember that next time you need a beating, Harold. (*Pause.*) I'll leave you to sort yourself out. And don't be too long about it.

Footsteps going out of the stable.
HAROLD's *renewed crying, at first in anger and frustration, then in a flood of released self-pity. The horses snicker and whinny softly on either side of him.*
Out of the horse-sounds emerge the voices of his mother and father.

VERA. Gently, now, son, gently. Don't cry anymore.

GEORGE. They brought us out of the darkness once a year . . . green slime.

HAROLD. I didn't mean to push you too hard.

VERA. Don't lie anymore. Make us proud of you.

GEORGE. They broke my back, crushed my ribs and smashed my hip-bone, Harold. But I can still work. Treat me right, and I can still work.

VERA. Gently, Harold, gently.

HAROLD. Don't grip the ayles too tight, don't force the furrow. Bring your big wheel up for deeper down, Dad. The breast of thy plough, the hymn says, glitters like an angel's wing. We'll stay together, won't we? Say we'll always stay together. You'll never leave me.

VERA. Gently, son, gently. Only beasts of burden.

GEORGE. Don't expect too much from labouring folk.

The voices of his mother and father merge back into the whinnying and snickering of the two horses.
Fade.

Fade in the foreman's office, and GRUNNIDGE.

GRUNNIDGE. . . . I'm not asking you, Perkins, I'm telling you. I want him out on field seven tomorrow with a two-horse hitch.

PERKINS. He's not ready yet. He's such a moody little bugger, Mr Grunnidge. You don't know when you've got him. It would go to his head.

GRUNNIDGE. I've got to get as much ploughing done as I can before the rain comes. Have you heard the weather forecast? Storms, and more storms. By the end of next week field seven will be a bog.

PERKINS. Well, God help the poor horses, I say.

GRUNNIDGE. Give people credit for learning, Perkins. Aren't you two hitting it off anymore?

PERKINS. He's not with the rest of us. Lives in his own world, day-dreaming. Talks in his sleep, thrashes about. (*Pause.*) I've been thinking of asking to share with someone else.

GRUNNIDGE. I'd take that as an admission of failure if I were you. Perseverance conquers, Perkins, not grumbling and grinding when things get difficult. I'm putting you up to third waggoner as from Monday.

PERKINS. Because of him? I don't want to get a leg up because of him. I want it on my own merit. You're bribing me, Mr Grunnidge. My pride won't let me take it.

GRUNNIDGE. It's not such a big, big thing, being third waggoner. Take the money, Perkins, and stop being such a twerp.

PERKINS. If he ever found out that you'd bribed me to stick it out with him . . . I'd go mad.

GRUNNIDGE. We all have a soft spot for something. With some its drink. With others its women. With me, it's the orphans of the plough. Spend your money wisely.

Fade.

Fade in the stable.
The sound of brushing and rubbing down of horses.

PERKINS (*fade in*). Good news for you, Harold.

HAROLD. What's that?

PERKINS. Promotion.

HAROLD. Don't be daft.

PERKINS. A friend of yours has been made third waggoner. How about that?

HAROLD. Oh, so *you've* been promoted. You don't deserve it.

PERKINS. Merit, Grunnidge said, pure merit. Doing well. Even with you round my neck.

HAROLD. You deserve a medal for that I've no doubt.

PERKINS. You're to take a two-horse hitch, and plough field seven tomorrow to a depth of ten inches. Get all the muck under. Left to right from the gate. Take Robin and Duster.

HAROLD. He's letting me out on my own? I thought it would be six months before I'd have another chance. Can't I take M . . . Bonny and Fred?

PERKINS. I told you which horses you could have. Robin and Duster. I'm using your favourites tomorrow if there's anything left after you've finished rubbing them down.

HAROLD. You're doing that to spite me.

PERKINS. That's right. Don't get too close to dumb animals, Harold. They don't understand.

HAROLD. They do.

PERKINS. See where you've got yourself? Go to church, Harold. Ask someone for some help.

HAROLD. If I say so — they won't work for you. All I've got to do is whisper it in their ears — don't pull for Joe Perkins — and they won't.

PERKINS. You're going mad, Harold.

HAROLD. I'll give you five shillings to let me take Bonny and Fred out tomorrow.

PERKINS. You haven't got five shillings.

HAROLD. I will have come next May. When I get paid out I'll give it to you.

PERKINS. That's more than a week's wages to you.

HAROLD. Take it.

PERKINS. I couldn't. Have the bloody horses. What's the difference to me?

Fade.

Fade in the open field.
The wind blowing. The horses àre standing, metal tinkling.

HAROLD. Now, I've got to get this perfect, Mum and Dad: straight furrows, every inch turned, no muck left on the surface. No wandering to one side now. Help me. I've got to show Grunnidge what I can do. Gee up.

The horses pull and the ploughing starts.

(*In his head:*) Cutting, not ripping and tearing. No great stones in this field, please God. I'm the man who makes the grass disappear, folding it in, tucking up the turf. Steady. Keep to the pattern. Leave no part of the land untouched. All the green has to go, Mum and Dad. All the green has to go.

Fade.

Fade in the foreman's office, and GRUNNIDGE.

GRUNNIDGE. . . . . they were all at some dinner or other, Harold, you know, a few brandies afterwards, a bit of bragging about his farm and his horses and his turnover. Then they got onto ploughing and our owner, bless his heart, spoke up and said he had the best ploughboy in the district and he'd back him to beat anyone under the age of eighteen in a match. Drunk as he was, he bet five guineas on you.

HAROLD. He should have made it ten.

GRUNNIDGE. Harold, you're only sixteen, son. There're lads on the other farms who've had two more years ploughing than you have for an under-eighteen match. Be circumspect in your boasting. Be humble, even.

HAROLD. When's the match?

GRUNNIDGE. Saturday morning.

HAROLD. Whose land?

GRUNNIDGE. Johnson's. I reckon I know which one he'll choose. It's on a fair slope and the clay is thicker at the bottom than the top. His ploughboy will have worked on it before.

HAROLD. Have we got a field anything like it I could practice on?

GRUNNIDGE. Near enough.

HAROLD. Does it need ploughing before Saturday?

GRUNNIDGE. Strange you should mention that. Bonny and Fred?

HAROLD. They'd do it blindfold. All I do is hang onto the back.

Fade.

Fade in a pub, and the MATCH JUDGE.

MATCH JUDGE. Gentlemen, I won't keep you waiting. My decision, after looking at that field and the various bits of ploughing by your boys, is that plot four was by far superior. I don't know who did plot four but all I can say is I wish he was working for me.

Applause. Fade.

A corridor nearby. Still the pub atmosphere.

GRUNNIDGE. That's thirty guineas the owner's won on you, Harold. He's very pleased.

HAROLD. So he should be.

GRUNNIDGE. They want to see you in there. Don't be too bold, son. The owner will give a guinea or even two. Take it with a smile and thank him.

HAROLD. He should be thanking me.

GRUNNIDGE. That's not how it works, Harold.

Fade.

The pub. The main bar, now noisier.
Fade in the OWNER.

OWNER. I'm very proud of you. Terrific display. Here's a guinea for you, boy. What's your name again?

HAROLD. Harold, sir. Thank you for the one guinea, sir.

OWNER. Harold is my champion! Watch out for him at the big show.

GRUNNIDGE. Would you like that: a crack at Southwell Ploughing Match?

HAROLD. If it's worth my while.

GRUNNIDGE. It is, if you win.

HAROLD. How much would I get?

GRUNNIDGE. Five pounds for first prize. Another couple from the owner if you remember your manners. That's half a year's wages at one hit. And then, Harold, there's the glory. Now you'd better get out and walk those horses home before the bobby catches you drinking.

HAROLD. There's nothing to beer. It has no effect on me at all.

GRUNNIDGE. Well, the rest of us are only human. It makes me quite cheerful after a dozen pints or so. Get out of here, you big-headed brat. The men are going to celebrate your victory.

Fade.

Fade in the atmosphere of country road. Two horses walking on a metalled surface.

HAROLD. I told you we'd win, Mum and Dad. It was no contest really. We're a good team and no one can beat that.

The sound of a bicycle bell and an approaching cycle.

PERKINS (*approaching*). You did it, Harold! What d'you say to the man who taught you everything you know? I had to work so I couldn't watch you. But they told me how great you were. Wiped the floor with them all.

HAROLD. Boss gave me a guinea, the mean old bugger.

PERKINS. That's not bad.

HAROLD. When I'd won him thirty!

PERKINS. There's a letter for you. I've left it on the bed.

HAROLD. A letter?

PERKINS. Yes, a real letter. On paper. With a stamp.

HAROLD. Do us a favour, Joe. Walk Mum and Dad home for me and lend us your bike.

PERKINS. Walk who home?

HAROLD. Come on, please! I want to read me letter.

PERKINS (*laughing*). Mum and Dad, is it? I get you. All right, Harold. Here, pedal off. But I'll expect you to treat me for this.

HAROLD. I will. I will.

HAROLD *pedals off, leaving the horses.*
The sound of wind in the hedgerows and the whirring of the wheels.

HAROLD (*in his head*). It'll be me mum's tracked me down. I knew she would. Wait till I tell her about today. And it will be one in the eye for Dad. Jesus, he'll look stupid when he finds out I'm winning . . .

Fade.

Fade in the dormitory and the sound of HAROLD *running, picking up the letter.*

HAROLD (*in his head*). Is that me mum's handwriting? I'd forgotten what it ever looked like . . .

The sound of the letter being torn open.
Fade the dormitory.
Fade in a special letter atmosphere.

YATES. Dear Harold Ransom,
    As I promised to let you know if I heard anything that could help you find your mother and father, I'm writing to say that Mr Ransom is

working at Egmanton for a man called Rice who employs him as a gardener at his private home. This is reliable information as I got it from the pit office who had to follow him through because of his insurance stamps.

I hope this is useful. There is no news of your mother.

Yours sincerely, Thomas Yates.

HAROLD (*in his head*). Egmanton. That's only a couple of miles from here. But what's he done with me mum?

Fade.

Fade in the stable. The horses are being groomed.

PERKINS. So who was your letter from?

HAROLD. A girl I used to go round with.

PERKINS. You must have started early. Love letters from women at your age. What did you do that they remember you so kindly?

HAROLD. Childhood sweetheart.

PERKINS. Childhood. That's ages ago with you, Harold. I sometimes think you've overtaken me in years. I've never had a leter from a woman. Had a man's hand, that girl who wrote to you. But then people in a pit village can't tell the difference between men and women, can they? Everyone's covered in coal-dust.

HAROLD. They're entering me for the Southwell Ploughing Match.

PERKINS. I expect they'll ask me to go in as well — in the senior class, of course.

HAROLD. I wouldn't mind taking on the over-eighteens. I wouldn't mind taking anyone on.

PERKINS. You won't get the blue rosette for modesty, Harold, that's for sure. Bonny needs a shoe.

HAROLD. I'll tell the waggoner.

PERKINS. Or is it Mum needs a shoe? (*Pause.*) It's all right, Harold. I won't tell on you.

HAROLD. If you want any ploughing lessons let me know.

PERKINS. Cheeky little beggar.

Fade.

Fade in a garden atmosphere. The sound of a gravel drive being raked. Birdsong. The crunching of boots on gravel. The raking continues. The boots stop.

HAROLD. Hello, Dad.

The raking stops.

GEORGE. What are you doing here?

HAROLD. I work at Laxton, not far away.

GEORGE. You've grown. How did you get over here?

HAROLD. I walked over.

GEORGE. Some have the time to walk.

The raking starts again.

HAROLD. Why did you leave the pit?

GEORGE. Mr Rice doesn't like gossiping. If I'm working, I'm working.

HAROLD. I went back to the house.

GEORGE. Still standing, is it.

HAROLD. There's someone called Yates living there now.

GEORGE. Keeping fit, are you? You seem all right.

HAROLD. What happened after I'd left? . . . I'm sorry I went like that.

GEORGE. You'd had enough. You flew the nest, that's all.

HAROLD. But you and Mum . . . I didn't know you'd break up.

GEORGE. That's nothing to do with you.

HAROLD. I'm your child! Both of yours' child . . .

GEORGE. Are you still a child? Is that what's standing in front of me?
It doesn't look like one.

HAROLD. I didn't want to lose touch.

GEORGE. Did you walk all that way to watch me raking gravel in a
rich man's drive? Was that worth it?

HAROLD. I've missed you both.

GEORGE. That won't help any of us now. You'll just have to manage
as best you can. (*Pause.*) Nobody should expect too much from
their parents.

HAROLD. I only wanted to see you.

GEORGE. Well, here I am. Got what you wanted?

HAROLD. I haven't seen you for over two years.

GEORGE. Is that something to complain about?

HAROLD. Where's Mum? Where's she got to?

GEORGE. Mr Rice is watching us through the window. That's all he's got
to do with himself.

HAROLD. I'll wait for you when you've finished.

GEORGE. You'll have a long wait.

HAROLD. There's a lot to talk about.

GEORGE. There's nothing to talk about. I don't know where your mother is.

The sound of a window opening nearby.

RICE (*calling*). Ransom! Who's that with you? Is he looking for work? Come here, boy!

GEORGE. Get off with you. You're getting me into bother.

HAROLD. I'll wait in the road.

GEORGE. You won't. Wait behind the last cottage on the left as you go out towards Kirton. But don't go in.

The garden atmosphere fades on the raking of gravel.

Fade in a field, and VALERIE.

VALERIE. Hey, what are you doing hanging around here, young man?

HAROLD. I'm waiting for someone.

VALERIE. Who are you waiting for?

HAROLD. For my dad.

VALERIE (*more tentatively*). What's his name?

HAROLD. The same as mine.

VALERIE. Is your name Ransom?

HAROLD. How did you guess?

VALERIE. Your manners are like his. You might as well come inside.

Fade.

Fade in a cottage parlour, and VALERIE.

VALERIE. You must know him, what he's like. Why should it surprise you? He never talks about people if he can help it.

HAROLD. He's never mentioned me? Never said he has a son?

VALERIE. No. Don't feel put out. He never mentions anybody.

HAROLD. I bet he mentions me mum.

VALERIE. Her least of all. Which you might expect, under the circumstances.

HAROLD. What d'you live with him for?

VALERIE. He's someone to have around.

HAROLD. But he's married to me mum.

VALERIE. She walked out, not him. If I thought he had a heart I'd say she broke it for him.

HAROLD. How did you meet him?

VALERIE. He was doing part-time gardening at the house where I was the cook. I had to feed him. He came into the kitchen every day he was there. I suppose I got used to looking after him.

HAROLD. Do you like living with him?

VALERIE. It's better than being on my own.

HAROLD. Does he know where me mum is? I've asked him and he says he doesn't, but he could be lying.

VALERIE. Your father speaks so seldom that he'd never bother to waste words on a lie.

The door opens and closes. The sound of footsteps entering the parlour.

GEORGE. I told you to wait outside and not come in here.

VALERIE. He was waiting round the back. I invited him in when I found out who he was. Do you want your tea?

GEORGE. He's my son. His name is Harold.

VALERIE. I didn't know his name was Harold.

GEORGE. He's over at Laxton. Can you give him some tea as well?

VALERIE. Yes. I'll get it now.

GEORGE. What are you doing over at Laxton?

HAROLD. Ploughing.

GEORGE. Ploughing. I sometimes wondered what you'd get up to.

HAROLD. I just won a ploughing match. I was competing with five others.

GEORGE. How far is it to walk?

HAROLD. If you plough an acre you have to walk eleven miles altogether.

GEORGE. I mean how far from Laxton?

HAROLD. I don't know. An hour or so on foot. I'm being entered for the Southwell Ploughing Match. The foreman says I might get sponsors interested if I win. I could go on, get big money.

GEORGE. Do they treat you right?

HAROLD. I could make seven pounds at one match if I win.

GEORGE. I said — do they treat you right? Do you get paid decent wages? Is it a good job where you work?

HAROLD. Not bad.

VALERIE. Do you like meat pie, Harold?

GEORGE *laughs wryly.*

HAROLD. I won't stay for tea. It's a long walk back and I have to shut up the chickens.

VALERIE. Don't go. It'll be on the table in a minute.

HAROLD. I must. Dad, do you know me granny's address in Rotherham?

GEORGE. Your mother's not there. I tried.

The door opens and closes quickly.

VALERIE. What was all that about?

GEORGE. A bit of history. If he comes again, don't serve him pie.

VALERIE. I thought we were getting on all right. I'd like to see him again. He looks like you.

GEORGE. That's something for him to worry about, not us.

VALERIE. I'd often wondered why we had to move up here . . .

GEORGE. I'll have me tea now, if that's all right.

VALERIE. Why don't you tell the lad that you care about him? Tell me, and all, while you're at it. Do you have to be so secretive?

GEORGE. Don't interfere, Valerie. He's my son, not thine.

VALERIE. Who needs telling? Being with you two in the same room is like watching a couple of goldfish in a bowl.

Fade.

Fade in a special atmosphere.

VERA. 14 Anderson Street, Dundee.   25th April 1931.
Dear Harold,
I am very sorry that it has taken me so long to write to you but I did not know where you were until your father sent a letter to your gran for her to forward it to me. I have been up here in Scotland for over two years now working in a commercial hotel. It is not a bad job except that the hours are long and I spend a lot of time on my feet. One day I will come down for a visit and you can show me round the farm. I never expected you to end up in that line, I must say . . .

Fade.

Fade in the country road. Footsteps.

HAROLD. Hello Dad. I've been waiting for you.

The footsteps continue, joined by HAROLD's, *and the ticking over of a bicycle being pushed.*

I kept out of Mr Rice's way. He didn't see me. I've had a letter from Mum.

The footsteps quicken. HAROLD's follow.

She says she's coming down for a visit.

GEORGE. Is that your bike?

HAROLD. No, I borrowed it.

GEORGE. See you take good care of it then.

HAROLD. Mum's in Scotland. Why did she go up there?

GEORGE. I don't want to know.

The footsteps stop.

HAROLD. But you wrote to her.

GEORGE. But I didn't know where she was. I just reckoned your granny would. I don't want to know where your mother is, and she doesn't want me to know. So, now I've been told it's Scotland. We'll leave it at Scotland. It's a big enough place.

HAROLD. If she comes down . . .

GEORGE. Don't bring her over here.

The footsteps and the bicycle resume.

HAROLD. I've been entered officially for the Southwell Ploughing Match. Perhaps you'll come and watch me.

GEORGE. There's no fun in watching other men work.

HAROLD. Mr Grunnidge thinks I'm in with a chance. All the big firms will be there looking for people to sponsor — Cooks of Lincoln, Ransom Sims and Jefferies of Ipswich, best ploughs you can get. Same name as us, Ransoms. Isn't that strange? Our owner's given me two days off, he's putting me up in a boarding-house, all paid . . . say you'll come . . .

GEORGE. What for?

HAROLD. So you'll see how I'm getting on . . . that I'm good at something.

GEORGE. You're bloody good at talking, I'll say that for you.

Pause.
The footsteps and bicycle sounds continue.

HAROLD. Can I come back home with you? Or will your . . . friend mind?

GEORGE. I'd rather you didn't.

HAROLD. Why?

GEORGE. That's none of your business.

HAROLD. I've done a day's work then got myself over to see you . . .

GEORGE. Without being asked.

HAROLD. I can see my own father if I want, can't I?

GEORGE. Well, now you've seen me. What do you find? I'm tired, Harold. I want to be quiet. So, don't torment me. (*Pause.*) Get on your bike and go back to Laxton. Come over next Sunday for your dinner if you like.

HAROLD. Thanks, Dad. I will, I will. The ploughing match is in two weeks.

The sound of the bicycle being mounted and ridden off, the bell being rung.

GEORGE (*to himself*). Scotland, eh. About as far as she could get.

Fade.

Fade in the stable. The sound of brushing of horses. Fade in HAROLD.

HAROLD. Got to make you beautiful for tomorrow, Mum and Dad. Everyone will be looking at you . . .

GRUNNIDGE. How are you doing, Harold?

HAROLD. Just bedding them down, Mr Grunnidge.

GRUNNIDGE. We're running that stallion close, you know.

HAROLD. He's all right.

GRUNNIDGE. We're into the season. I shouldn't have let you take him with the mare. It could ruin your chances if he starts to play up.

HAROLD. He won't. He's as firm as a rock.

GRUNNIDGE. You won't stop him if he gets the idea into his head. I don't want us looking fools in front of all Southwell and district.

HAROLD. I feel lucky, Mr Grunnidge. I don't think I'll have any trouble.

GRUNNIDGE. Get a good night's sleep. No sloping off to the alehouse. Come to think of it, I'll get you some whisky to do their coats with in the morning. Makes them shine, Harold. I love that. Two shining horses, and a shining plough. Is your father coming to watch?

HAROLD. He said he'd try . . . it's the bloke he works for, Mr Rice . . . he's not likely to give him time off.

GRUNNIDGE. That's a pity. You should have mentioned it to me. I know Mr Rice. He's only an old solicitor from Newark. I've done business with him before he retired.

HAROLD. He's a hard task-master, my dad says. On his back all the time. Wants his pound of flesh.

GRUNNIDGE. Doesn't sound like the man I know, but I'll take your word for it. Don't be long out of bed now. Goodnight.

HAROLD. Goodnight. (*Pause.*) You won't let me down tomorrow, will you, Dad. No nonsense, no being carried away, or biting, or kicking . . . just side by side, with Mum, together.

Fade.

Fade in an open field: the ploughing match.
A megaphoned voice.

VOICE. . . . and on plot nine, Harold Ransom of Laxton Common with a pair of Shires, Bonny and Fred . . .

The megaphoned voice fades.

HAROLD (*in his head*). Small wheel set for forty-five degrees. Coulter and share a penny's-width apart. No slack in the reins. Everything is firm. We're ready, Mum and Dad.

(*In the atmosphere:*) Gee up!

The horses pull the plough. The share cuts into the ground and sends up the first seam of earth off the breast.

(*In his head:*) We're well set in. Open the rig out, turn, close the rig, keeping the line, always keeping the line . . .

Ploughing sound effects at a greater distance.
Fade in GRUNNIDGE.

GRUNNIDGE. . . . don't ask me how he does it. He's a bad-tempered, awkward little beggar is our Harold, very stiff-necked, Mr Manley, but if you want to sell ploughs for your company, take Harold on to sponsor him.

MANLEY. Will he win today?

GRUNNIDGE. Watch him. He's only been up and down the plot four times and it looks as though he's drawn those furrows with a ruler. When he's finished it will look like a geometry exercise. I've never seen such regular, even ploughing.

MANLEY. He must have been well taught by someone.

GRUNNIDGE. No. The man he spent most of his time with will struggle all his life to get halfway to Harold's standard.

MANLEY. What's he got then? Is it temperament? Doesn't sound like it. Strong wrists? Or does he just like staring at horses' backsides?

GRUNNIDGE. It's the place where he loses himself.

HAROLD (*in his head*). Don't keep looking at her, Dad. I should have put the blinkers on you both. Put your head down, Dad!

MANLEY. Your stallion is starting to act up. Left it a bit late to have him hitched to a mare, haven't you?

GRUNNIDGE. That's Harold's team. Defying nature is natural to him.

MANLEY. They'll run away with him if he's not careful.

GRUNNIDGE. I don't think so. The plough is what matters and it's cutting perfect seams in perfect shapes, no matter what's going on ahead of it. Harold has his hand on all the vibrations.

Fade.

HAROLD (*in his head*). Don't keep banging into her with your shoulder, you stupid, bloody brute! If you bite her I'll whip you with these reins until you bleed!

Special atmosphere.

GEORGE. Hit me, son, go on, hit me. But it won't stop me doing anything I want to.

VERA. . . . I have to spend a lot of time on my feet.

VALERIE. . . . don't go. It'll be on the table in a minute.

GEORGE. It's time for me to hurt her, Harold. You can't do anything about it.

VERA. . . . so long to write to you. So long to write to you.

Fade the special atmosphere.
Fade in the ploughing sounds.

GRUNNIDGE. Keep it up, Harold! You've got it like lines in an exercise book! Watch out for Fred though. He's getting nasty.

HAROLD. I've got him well in hand, Mr Grunnidge. He won't get away from me.

Fade.

Fade in the stable. Restless horses clattering and snorting.
Fade in GRUNNIDGE.

GRUNNIDGE. I want to introduce you to Mr Manley who's the chief salesman for Ransom, Sims and Jefferies of Ipswich. He'd like a word with you.

MANLEY. Congratulations, Harold. That's as good as I've seen for a long time. You came out a worthy winner.

GRUNNIDGE. Harold, straighten up now and talk to the gentleman.

HAROLD. We must get the horses separated, Mr Grunnidge. He's going to kick the stable down.

GRUNNIDGE. Don't you worry. I'll deal with the horses. Have a talk to Mr Manley and remember, he's offering you some help you could do with.

HAROLD. Those two have nearly yanked my arms out of their sockets.

I'm aching all over. He'd have bitten her in half if I'd let him, the sod.

MANLEY. Don't know how you controlled them. Come on, we'll have a drink somewhere. Mr Grunnidge can catch up with us later.

GRUNNIDGE. Lemonade only for him. He's under eighteen, remember.

MANLEY. It's the All England under-eighteen Ploughing Championship I want to discuss with him — so, lemonade it will be.

Fade.

Fade in a kitchen atmosphere, the sound of many people working.
Fade in HAROLD.

HAROLD. Mrs Ransom.

COOK. What's her first name?

HAROLD. Vera.

COOK. What d'you want her for?

HAROLD. I'm her son.

COOK. We're in the middle of doing lunch at the moment. She can't be spared.

HAROLD. I've come up all the way from Newark on the train to see her.

COOK. Go and amuse yourself till half-past four when she gets a break. You'll find her out the back with the rest getting a breath of fresh air.

HAROLD. Don't tell her I'm here, I want it to be a surprise.

COOK. Oh, she'll be ready for a surprise by then. Go on, you're in the way . . .

Fade.

Fade in rear of hotel open atmosphere.
A group of hotel workers chatting.

HAROLD (*whispering*). Mum.

VERA. Harold! How did you get here?

HAROLD. I came on the train.

VERA. This is my son, Harold.

COOK. We've met.

HAROLD. You're smoking, Mum. You didn't used to.

VERA. Come on, we'll go for a walk.

COOK. Back here for five, Vera.

VERA (*under her breath*). Oh, shut up, will you.

HAROLD. I hardly recognised you. You've lost a lot of weight.

VERA. It's the Scottish way of working, Harold. You run everyone into the ground.

HAROLD. D'you mind me coming?

VERA. I was coming down to see you in a month or so, when I'd got some money together.

HAROLD. I can give you some money if you like.

VERA. Well-off now, are you? How did you get rich?

HAROLD. I'm not rich but I save. And I've won a couple of ploughing competitions. I got seven pounds for the last one.

VERA. Ploughing competitions. What are you doing in ploughing competitions? Doesn't sound like my Harold. Baking pies, perhaps. You got my letter, then.

HAROLD. Yes. I didn't write back because I couldn't sort out what to say.

VERA. That's a bit too like your father for comfort.

HAROLD. I look like him, don't I?

VERA. More and more.

HAROLD. A man should look more like his dad than his mum, surely?

VERA. Oh, aye.

HAROLD. When are you coming down to see us then?

VERA. I'm seeing you now, aren't I?

HAROLD. You can see Dad as well. He lives only a couple of miles away from the farm where I work.

VERA. How is he?

HAROLD. He has a job as a gardener.

VERA. At least that's something he can do. Better than hanging around the pit doing half-jobs.

HAROLD. When are you coming down, then.

VERA. Well, I'll have to think about that.

HAROLD. Can you make it in September?

VERA. Why September?

HAROLD. I'm competing in the All-England Ploughing Match at Lincoln. You could come and watch me win.

VERA. Oh, so you're going to win, are you? You know that already.

HAROLD. Only the under-eighteen section. They won't let me take on the seniors.

VERA. I bet they're relieved to hear that. You're very cocky these days.

HAROLD. You could come and live near Laxton. I could stay with you and give you my wages for the housekeeping. There're lots of cottages vacant.

VERA. But you're on your own now, Harold. You don't want to be living with your mother at your age.

HAROLD. We could meet Dad now and then.

VERA. I'll try and come down for a week in September. Do you know the date of this ploughing thing?

HAROLD. The tenth. But come down on the ninth so we can travel to Lincoln together. They'll put you up, if I ask them.

VERA. Who's they?

HAROLD. My sponsors. They're big farming machinery manufacturers. Ransom, Sims and Jefferies. They'd do anything for me.

Fade.

Fade in the parlour of the Egmanton cottage, and HAROLD.

HAROLD. September the tenth, at Lincoln. If you ask Mr Rice now, give him some notice, he'd let you have a couple of days off.

GEORGE. Would he now? You seem to know a lot about the way his mind works.

HAROLD. Our foreman knows him. He says he's not a bad sort.

GEORGE. Your foreman doesn't work for him.

VALERIE. Ask the old misery if you can go. It'll do you good. We can have a holiday. I'd like to go to Lincoln.

HAROLD. Oh . . . I was meaning that Dad could come with me . . . stay in the boarding house . . . my sponsors would gladly pay for him but I don't think they'd run to two of you . . .

VALERIE. I could pay for myself.

HAROLD. If they knew who you were . . . that you weren't my mother . . .

VALERIE. I see.

HAROLD. It'll be my big day, Dad.

GEORGE. Sounds like it. Have you heard from your mother?

HAROLD. No. I'll write to her some time.

Fade.

Fade in the dormitory, and PERKINS.

PERKINS. You can have the bed to yourself now, Harold. If they take on a new boy now you're fourth waggoner and I'm leaving, I'd suggest you tell Grunnidge that you've got some terrible skin disease so you can sleep by yourself. Since you and I have shared that bed I've never had more than three hours proper sleep in a night.

HAROLD. What are you going to do with yourself, Joe?

PERKINS. Won't be farming. I thought about joining the army.

HAROLD. Doing what?

PERKINS. Anything, so long as it's nothing to do with horses. Ride a motorbike, drive a lorry, I don't care. I'm fed up with this kind of life. This place is behind the times.

HAROLD. Grunnidge is getting a tractor next year.

PERKINS. He's been saying that ever since I came to Laxton. He's not a tractor man. Too old, Harold, too old. Tractors are part of the future. That's why you're wasting your time with these ploughing competitions. It's from a bygone age, all that stuff. You're playing games.

HAROLD. You'd have been interested if you'd have been good enough.

PERKINS. What? Put all that time and energy into something as simple as ploughing? Talking to horses? Listen, Harold, the daftest bloke alive can plough. Anyone can plough. It's simple.

HAROLD. Why couldn't you do it as well as I could, then?

PERKINS. Wasn't worth it. Mum and Dad. What was all that about? Calling a couple of stupid horses your mum and dad.

HAROLD. I don't do that anymore. I was just playing . . . because . . . well, I was young. You never told anyone, did you?

PERKINS. I said I wouldn't, didn't I?

HAROLD. Do you want to know if I win or not in September?

PERKINS. Oh, it will be all over the papers, I expect. Front page headlines. 'Our Harold Does It Again.' (*Pause.*) Send me a postcard.

HAROLD. Where to?

PERKINS. Care of the dole office. Ta-ra.

Fade.

Fade in the open field at the All-England Match, Lincoln, and GRUNNIDGE.

GRUNNIDGE. This is it then, Harold. There's your plot, you've set your plough, all you have to do is win. Second nature to you now, I should think, isn't it?

HAROLD. I thought me mum and dad would be here to watch me.

GRUNNIDGE. I know, son. You must be disappointed. But I expect they're busy. I'm here, aren't I?

HAROLD. You're not family.

GRUNNIDGE. Near enough.

HAROLD. I wanted them to be here. I don't know who I'm doing this for, Mr Grunnidge.

GRUNNIDGE. I could say, the pride and the glory: I could say Ransom, Sims and Jefferies: I could say our farm, our owner, bless him: I could say me — but . . . it must be for thee, son. You've mastered something. Show them.

HAROLD. I'll never forgive them for this. Even if I win, and I will, by God, I will, I'll not speak to those two again as long as I live. Gee up!

The plough starts moving.
Fade.

Fade in the dormitory, and GRUNNIDGE.

GRUNNIDGE. What standard of production have we got for Plough Monday then? Have you got your lines learnt?

STAN. We're struggling with them, Mr Grunnidge. Harold keeps forgetting.

GRUNNIDGE. Which part are you playing, Harold.

HAROLD. I wanted to do Saint George but they've got me on the Doctor.

GRUNNIDGE. Old Et Essum Squocum. I did him a few times. Doctor, doctor, five pound for a doctor. I'll give you ten to stay away.

HAROLD. You can do it if you like.

GRUNNIDGE. I'm too old to go pulling a plough around. There's snow on the way according to the feller on the weather forecast. Where are you going to go with your play?

STAN. All round here. Harold says we might try Egmanton. Depends how well we do. If no one lets us in to do it we might get fed up and go down the pub.

GRUNNIDGE. No, you must take your play out on Plough Monday. It's always been done. New Year wouldn't be the same without it. Plenty of folk will let you in, and be open-handed.

Fade.

Fade in the farmhouse.
A small crowd of people in a good mood.
Fade in the ploughboys.

PLOUGHBOYS. Good master, and good mist-er-ess,
　As you sit by the fire,
　Pray think of us poor plough lads
　That plough through mud and mire.
　We're not the London actors
　That act upon the stage,
　We're just the country plough lads,
　That plough for little wage.
　We've done our best that best can do
　And best can do no more,
　We wish you all good night, good luck,
　And another happy year.

　Applause.

FARMER. Well spoken, lads. Brandy is the only reward for such
　artistry. I've never heard that play done better — even by Henry Irving.

　Laughter; the clink of glasses.
　Fade.

Fade in a country road. The sound of horses pulling a cart containing the
ploughboys and the plough. Fade in STAN.

STAN. But this is a private house, Harold, not a farm. We're only
　supposed to go round the farms.

HAROLD (*quite drunk*). It's a big enough house, isn't it? There's farms
　all around. Get the plough out of the cart and I'll knock the old
　bugger up.

STAN. I don't think we should. If he's not a farmer he won't know what
　we're doing.

HAROLD. The rule is, if anyone turns us down and won't let us perform
　in their house, and won't give us a few bob, a bit to eat and a beer . . .
　he pays a forfeit. Anybody. Not just farmers. Anybody. Mr Rice, who
　lives here, has people tilling his land. I know that. I'll sort him out.

　Fade.

　Knocking.

HAROLD (*to himself*). Come on, Rice. Open the bloody door.

　The door is unbolted and opened.

RICE. Yes? What do you want?

HAROLD. We've come to do our play. Let us in.

RICE. Who is 'we', may I ask?

HAROLD. We're ploughboys from Laxton. It's Plough Monday, today, in case you hadn't noticed.

RICE. No, I hadn't. And, I must say, I don't like your tone.

HAROLD. I couldn't care less. You're a tight-arsed old bastard.

RICE. I think you'd better go. You're drunk.

HAROLD. You're turning us down. You won't let us in to do our play?

RICE. Certainly not. Now get off my property.

HAROLD. Right. Thank you very much indeed.

> *Fade.*
> *Fade in STAN.*

STAN. Aw, come on, Harold. We don't need to make him pay a forfeit. He's not one of us . . .

HAROLD. He threw me out. He broke the rule. Get everyone in those traces. You lot are going to be my horses.

STAN. What are you going to do?

HAROLD. Plough up his bloody lawn.

STAN. He'll see us.

HAROLD. Not in snow this thick, he won't. And I don't make a lot of noise when I plough. That's one thing you learn when you're an All-England champion. You don't make much noise. You just do it.

> *Fade.*
> *The slight tinkling of the plough.*
> *The heavy breathing of boys pulling the plough.*
> *The sound of share cutting the turf.*

STAN (*breathless — whispering*). How are we getting on, Harold?

HAROLD. A yard or so left, that's all.

STAN. You've made a neat job of it.

HAROLD. It's coming over like roast beef off a knife.

> *Fade.*
> *Fade in.*

HAROLD. We'll stack all the turfs against his front door so when he opens it in the morning, he'll get the lot fall in on him.

STAN. Hell, Harold, that's going too far. He'll have the bobby onto us.

HAROLD. Ploughboys never get done for Plough Monday forfeits round here. And Rice is an offcomer anyway. No one will listen to him.

STAN. When did you dream this up?

HAROLD. It just came into my head. Get working.

> *Fade.*

Knocking.

HAROLD. Come on, Rice. Shift yourself. I'm freezing out here. Ooooh, what a night, what a night.

The door opens.

Hell, Mr Rice! What are you doing in your house?

RICE. I told you to go away.

HAROLD. Well, I thought as I'd tried the front door first time I'd better come round the back and see if I had better luck. It's a good play we've got for you. The best actors for miles. All we want is ten pounds, a bottle of brandy, no, make that two . . .

RICE. I'm going to call the police.

HAROLD. I'm your gardener's son.

RICE. I thought I'd seen you before.

HAROLD. Harold Ransom, son of George Ransom, not so you'd notice. I expect you'll have to fire him now, won't you?

RICE. Step inside for a moment.

HAROLD. Not likely.

RICE. Have you seen your father lately?

HAROLD. No. I never see him. He's lost his job now, hasn't he? I've stopped him . . . like he stopped me . . . I hate him, Mr Rice.

RICE. Your father doesn't work here anymore. He left my employment at the end of September to go to Scotland.

HAROLD. Scotland.

RICE. We'll forget all about tonight. I can see you're upset. I think you should get back home now. This is becoming quite a blizzard. Good night.

The door closes.

HAROLD. Scotland.

PLOUGHBOYS. In comes I, the ploughman,
    Don't you see my whip in hand,
    As I go forth to plough the land
    To turn it downside up?
    Straight I go from end to end,
    I scarcely make a bulk or bend,
    Then to my horses I attend,
    With Gee, whoa, back and arve.

HAROLD. It wasn't all that bad . . . Scotland . . . I could go mining now, of my own accord . . . live close by, not too close but . . . close enough to call in. They'll be glad to see me. Yes, I'll go to Scotland . . .

MENOCCHIO

by James Saunders

For Freddie Jones

James Saunders was born in London in 1925. He has been writing radio plays since the fifties. The most recent include *Random Moments in a May Garden*, *Nothing to Declare*, *The Flower Case*, and his latest, *The Magic Bathroom*. For television he wrote the comedy series, *Bloomers*, and has adapted stories by, among others, D.H. Lawrence, Henry James, H.E. Bates, V.S. Pritchett, and Somerset Maugham, including the television film of Lawrence's *The Captain's Doll*. He was awarded an Arts Council Bursary in 1960, and a Major Bursary in 1984. His stage play, *Next Time I'll Sing to You*, won the 1963 Evening Standard Drama Award. Other full-length plays include *A Scent of Flowers*, *The Italian Girl*, *Hans Kohlhaas*, *Bodies*, *Fall*, and *A Journey to London*. He has also written many one-act plays.

Menocchio was first broadcast on BBC Radio 3 on 19 January 1985, with Freddie Jones as Menocchio.

Director: Richard Wortley
Running time, as broadcast: 59 minutes 56 seconds.

In the name of the Father and of the Son and of the Holy Spirit.

I, Domenico Scandella, called Menocchio of Montereale, am a baptised Christian and have lived always in a Christian way according to my judgement, and have performed Christian works, and I have always been obedient to my superiors and to my spiritual fathers, to the best of my ability, and always, morning and night, I crossed myself with the sign of the holy cross saying, 'In the name of the Father and of the Son and of the Holy Spirit.' And I recited the Pater Noster and the Ave Maria and the Credo with a prayer to Our Lord and one to the Madonna.
It is indeed the case that I thought and believed and said, as it will show in the records of my trials, things against the commandments of the Church. It is also the case that I said some things at my trials that were not true in fact and some that were not true in spirit. In making these lies and evasions, I see now that I did a wrong thing, which was a sin against the truth and against my own nature, as well as wasting the time of the holy fathers, for which I beg their forgiveness.

But I must say something else about that. When the learned Inquisitors caught me out in one of these contradictions of myself, they did not say 'You are lying, Menocchio,' or 'Menocchio, you are talking nonsense', but led me on further with more questions which they asked with a kindly expression and their brows furrowed as if all they wanted in the world was to understand my true meaning, and the more I tried to answer their questions the more I fell into confusion until, like a man, you could say, had up before a clever magistrate for stealing a pig or a round of cheese, who pleads that he did not steal the cheese but meant to give it back afterwards, and that he took it because he was hungry and ate it, and that he did not take the cheese but someone else did and it was not a cheese at all but a ham — so did I tie myself up hand and foot with contradictions — tie my mouth I should say, until I was so tied up I had to fall silent. But I want to say that when this happened, though I seemed to be like a hare running this way and that across a field to escape its hunters — and I know the holy fathers took it

to be that — it was *not* only that but also, many times, that I was darting
in my mind back and forth trying to make some sense of what had come
into my head that I truly at the time believed or at least found it
interesting to think about. And that this kind of confusion — I am saying
now — came out of the position I found myself in, a humble miller —
which was my main occupation — with no chance until my trials of
sharpening the ideas that came into my head against the experience and
learning of the church fathers, but only against the dull wits of simple
country people, and the few people I could argue with I saw little of.
You can see from one or the other of my trials, I forget which, that a
witness from Montereale said that I once told him, 'If only I had the
chance to argue my ideas with princes and prelates and other wise men,
their eyes would fly open.' Or something of the kind. Well, I had my run
with those whose brains and learning fly as high above mine as a hawk above
a coney, and who saw me, I daresay, as the hawk would see the coney,
or I would say a fieldmouse, a slow small thing pressing its belly to the
ground, praying not to be noticed or, if noticed, to be left in peace as
too small for the hawk's concern. But things did not go that way, neither
to be left alone with my ideas nor to convince anyone they were worth
having nor even that whatever their worth I did no harm having them.
And I think now I was something of an ass to ever hope otherwise. I see
now there is a greater error in the world than any the holy fathers tried
to convince me of, a greater by far but which they, with all their piety
and learning, do not understand. I know that it is a sin to feel bitterness
toward the world, and I pray to God to relieve me of it before I die; but
it is what I feel, and I know no truth now but what I feel and what I
think, and I wish here, now I am come to my end, to write the truth.

   When they brought me here after my sentence was delivered, I asked
if I might have pen and paper to write letters to my family and friends.
Which they agreed though they said I must write nothing blasphemous,
nor anything touching on my trial, nor give vent to any of my ideas, nor
any criticisms of my treatment or of the court; that I might express my
sorrow at the pass I had brought myself to, so long as I expressed it with
the contrite heart of one confessing his sins and wishing to atone for
them. And that they would read the letters before they were passed out.
Well, they can do nothing more to me now, since a man can only die
once. Though I pray to the Almighty and Merciful God that it is not the
fire. I pray it is not the fire, I do not think I could — I was going to write
I do not think I could stand that, but if it is the way they choose, and it
is the usual way, then stand it I must and shall. But I hope it will be
quick. When they put me to the torture after my second trial, the
strappado, I could not stand that, though they said it was mild, I cried
out, 'I'll tell you names', and they let me down, this was the second time
they hung me up. And though I told them only the name of our local
lord, still if they had hung me up a third time I think I might have given
them all the names I could think of. But I can give names in this, since
they will not get hold of it. I hope they will let me have visitors, and that
someone will come. They are not badly disposed to me here. It has been

some months since the sentence, I do not know how many, except that it has gone very cold, and it was August when the trial ended; I think it is November now. I thought of scratching the days on the wall, but then I said to myself, 'Menocchio, does the date of your death matter to you? They will know it and keep it, you'll not be late for it, you'll not miss the meeting through not knowing the date.' I have been told that the people here, that is the Inquisitor of Concordia, does not want to have me killed, but that the Holy Office in Rome itself orders that they must, because it is the second time for me. Perhaps I should be proud that the Pope knows of my case. The first time I was three years in a dungeon, then they let me out on condition that I did not leave my village, Montereale, and wore always over my clothes the habitello with the painted cross, and kept my mouth shut. Which I did as far as I could for a number of years, but then sometimes I put the habitello on under something else, and my mouth would not stay shut forever. It would not. But I will write about that later on. If they let me have visitors, and someone comes, I will give him this to take out, though I do not know who will come to see me now. What he should do with it I do not know, just so that it goes out from this place. My eldest son, the one good apple in a basket of bad ones, is dead, and so is my wife, God rest them both. For the others, I think they will be glad when it is over and they can forget me, and how can I blame them, I brought them nothing good and more shame than money. When I was put in prison the first time, which by the sentence of the court was to be for my natural life, my family was ordered to pay for my keep there, which could not have endeared me to them. And being so far from Montereale, my wife could not visit me as otherwise she would have done, I'm sure, though Ziannuto came many times, my eldest son, and tried to help me in many other ways, getting a lawyer for me and putting about that I was mad so that they might let me go, this was before the trial, my first trial. But I did not mean to get to this so soon.

My name is Domenico Scandella, called Menocchio. To begin at the beginning, I was born in the village of Montereale, which is in the Friuli near the mountains, in the Year of Our Lord 1532 and, it being now 1599, my age is sixty-seven. And unlikely to increase further. You could say that I have come to a good age and if I do not live out the three score and ten allotted to us in the Bible, I can part easily enough with the other three. Only it be not the fire. I wonder they lived so long in those days, I could say it was that they were more righteous then, only it is not righteousness I think that stretches out the life, but an easy living of it, to judge by the gentlemen and lords, and priests too, who live some of them to a great age and the others I daresay kill themselves early with over-indulgence. And this, my sixty-seven years, in spite of the three years in prison that nearly killed me, I was not young then but somewhere in my fifties, and the dungeon in which they kept me so damp and dark and cold, as I stated in the letter I wrote pleading for my release, that I think the very look of me when I came before them was enough to tell them I could do no more harm if they let me free. Though

I want to say here that I never to my knowledge did harm to any man or woman, nor ever set out to. Except on one occasion, which was when I broke the arm of Francesco Fasseta, or rather he broke his own arm when he fell, and that was of his doing, as I told the magistrates, because it went this way: Francesco Fasseta, whom I forgive with all others who set out to hurt me, was one of those who, not having minds and thoughts of their own, copy whatever they hear and bandy it about without thinking; and there being as you may know a kind of story in the country which says all millers are rogues, so, when I took over the mill from my father, he accused me of keeping back some of his millet and giving him short measure, though he could not have believed it because I did no such thing nor ever have with anyone. And I told him to go away from in front of my mill and not cause trouble, and then he said, in front of everyone there, that he hoped I'd not turn out to be as big a rogue as my father had been. But I let this go too, because as I said at my first trial, when they asked why I had told someone blasphemy didn't matter, if a man blasphemes or says bad things to his neighbour he may hurt himself but he surely cannot hurt God, who being all intelligence is not to be put down by it; neither does it harm the man's neighbours, and if we do not hurt our neighbours we do not commit sin. So, instead of laying hands on him, I simply told him he was making an ass of himself in front of the others, who knew well enough who to listen to, and who also knew, if it came to fathers, how his own father had thrown him out of the house for interfering with his sister. Which I know for a fact to be true because the sister told me so. Whereupon he tried to lay hands on *me*. And after a while I threw him down and his arm broke. But this was a long time ago, more than thirty years ago, and not worth remembering. Even so, twenty years later this same Francesco Fasseta testified against me at my first trial, saying I'd told him when a man died his soul went back to the earth. Which is more or less what I did tell him, but he had no call to repeat it, or any of the other things he'd heard me say, and getting them wrong in the process because of the thickness of his head. And not just him but three others of the Fasseta family, they all came up to testify, and all on account of breaking his arm that time. Because some of them were there when it happened, and there was a general rumpus. And because the Fassetas were thick as thieves with the parish priest at that time, Don Odorico Vorai, with whom I'd had disagreements until finally I refused to have him confess me but went to Giovanni Melchiori instead in Polcenigo. He was the one, this Odorico Vorai, who put the Inquisition onto me, together with another priest, Don Ottavio Montereale, put up to it I daresay by the Fassetas. But my family had their own back, because while I was in prison they drove him out of the village, which was a good riddance since he was not much of a priest and a stupid man with it. As for the things they said I'd said, such as the soul returning to the earth, I want you to understand that some of these ideas were very complicated in my head and I put them out as simply as possible to the people in the village who for the most part could neither read nor write.

And also, I will admit, sometimes I said things to goad them, to make them argue with me, such as, 'God is just a puff of air,' or 'How can the Host be the body of Christ when you can see it's a lump of dough?' But all they'd say was, 'How can you know better than the Pope?' or 'Get away from me, Menocchio, I don't want to hear such things.' And then, when I had my chance to argue my ideas with the learned priests of the court, I made a pig's dinner of it. But I want to write about all that later on. But you must not think I got on badly with the villagers. This was not so. Even with the Fassetas there was no trouble most of the time, a man must rub along with his neighbours whatever kind of people they are, and however stupid, or life is not worth the living, and too I had my mills to run. And I was not just a miller, but on occasion carpenter, sawyer, mason or whatever else came up, so that I met with people a great deal and was respected, which I can prove since I was at one time mayor of the village and twice *camararo* of the church, which meant looking after all its affairs, the second time after I came back from prison, while I was still wearing the yellow cross. Also, on the occasion when Bastian de Martin was in dispute with our landlord, Count Giovan di Montereale, over the house and fields he was renting, which was to do with improvements he said he'd made to the place, which he said was a pigsty when he took it, and he should be let off some rent for the time and trouble he'd spent, I was called in to take Bastian's side and argue his case for him, which I think I did very well and saved him some money, even though I had my doubts about his side of it. This too came after I served my prison time. I write all this not from vanity but to give a picture of my position in the village.

I had two mills outside Montereale, both rented, whatever they say about millers I was not well off, though not so poor as most in the village. And two fields which I worked and grazed, also not mine. And in that village I lived all my life, apart from the years in prison in Concordia and the two years when I was banished from Montereale by the magistrate because of the trouble with Francesco Fasseta. And this time now. And I had by the time of my first trial seven children living, the eldest this Ziannuto, now dead, to my great sorrow. About the others I'll say nothing more.

I want to write now about my ideas, or thoughts or phantasies or whatever you wish to call them, and how they came into my head and why, if I had to have them, instead of keeping them to myself I went around arguing the toss about them, putting myself in danger as I must have known, because I was warned a number of times, mostly by priests, as it was stated at my first trial when our curate, Andrea Bionima, who was not a bad fellow, said he'd told me if I carried on saying such things I'd live to regret it. But I put no blame on Bionima, who said what he said at the trial to cover himself, the priests who started it off being as I said Don Odorico Vorai and Don Ottavio Montereale, this Don Ottavio being of the Count's family and knowing nothing about me but what he got at second hand from people like the Fassetas and from Vorai. It was Bionima the curate who lent me a book he'd found somewhere

about the travels of Zuanne de Mandevilla because he knew I liked to
read and the book was not on the list, and if he said at the hearing that
he'd not lent it to me but someone must have taken it from his house,
well, he would, wouldn't he? It was this book, this Mandevilla, which
caused me so much trouble when I read it, I was like the hunter's dog
when he started up two or three hares at once from a thicket and doesn't
know which to chase first. But I will write about that later, because it
was not from this book I began to have my thoughts, nor from any
book at that time but from my own observations of the world as far
as I knew it, my small world you can say since I'd not been farther than
Venice, nor ever have, nor will now, whereas the Mandevilla when
I read it covered the Holy Land and Jerusalem with all its different
sorts of Christian, and lands and islands even farther off, even as far as
Cathay and all the different races on earth but who all, says the book,
believe in the same one God even if they have the heads of dogs or
are like the race of pygmies who are a race of very little people but of
perfect shape, who look down on people of our size thinking them
grotesque; but all of them, says the book, are children of the same God
and are beloved of him, though they worship him in different ways. But
at this time I am writing about I knew nothing of any of this and read very
few books, not even the Holy Bible, which I did not have in the Italian
language till later on, and then it was not mine but I borrowed it from
time to time from my cousin Bastian, until Bastian's wife, when my
trial was coming up, took fright and burnt it in the oven. And though
I was three years in prison and am now here condemned, as a heretic and
backslider, I could never have put a Bible in the oven whatever language
it was written in. So as soon as I heard about it, I went round there as
fast as I could, being very angry and upset, so that Bastian could hardly
keep up with me, he being not much of a man in either body or intellect,
with a limp from falling off a roof when he was seven and the bones
setting wrong because his father was too mean to call in a doctor. And I
told her she was a stupid woman, and why did she not wrap it up in a
skin and bury it if she was so afraid of it and leave it to priests to burn
books, with Bastian standing hunched in the corner not knowing what
part to play since he was really on my side but afraid of his wife Fior,
who was as big as she was stupid, and I think knocked him about from
time to time. So he said nothing, while I told her she'd committed a
great sin and would go to hell for it, which I didn't believe since I don't
believe in hell nor ever have been able to, and I don't think the priests
do either in their hearts, judging from their behaviour. This was repeated
in court, of course, how I'd said it was a sin to burn that Bible, which
went against me, it being a prohibited book. But in the days I am trying
to write about I read few books, not realising what treasure they
contained. Now you must know how the country people have a way of
complaining about the world, saying such things as: 'The lords make the
laws, but we make the bread to fill their bellies', or 'Why do priests look
forward to heaven when they do so well on earth?', which you might
think was the beginning of a philosophy and a questioning of their lives,

but this is not so, any more than when they grumble about the rain or
a bad harvest or the cheese not going right, and there is no more
questioning in their grumbles than in the grumbling of their stomachs
when they are hungry. But I did not see things that way. If something
seemed to me to be wrong, it also seemed to me that it should be put
right, and as soon as possible. I told them so, trying to get them to argue
about the world and how it could be made better. But this was not
what they wanted, and they moved away or told me to hold my tongue.
Or they'd groan and say, 'Why bother to have a millwheel, Menocchio,
you could grind the corn with your jaw.' And this is when I started
making myself something of a buffoon.

It was later on that I started to think not just about this world but
about the other one, and not just about the priests and their privileges
but about the things they'd have us believe. And it went this way:
after I came to see that the priests were like another kind of lord over
us, owning much of the land and living off the tithes they took from
us — and if we didn't pay them they could excommunicate us — I started
to wonder how this had come about, since I was sure they'd not won
what they had by fighting for it. This I never did understand, and none
of the books I read since has anything to say of it. So I thought: 'Well,
how the priests got their power makes no difference, since they've got
it. A better question is, how do they keep it?' And that was an easy one
to answer. Because, while the lords put themselves above us with their
money and the law, the priests do it by putting it about that without
their knowledge and wisdom we stand no chance of getting into Heaven,
as if only they have hold of the key to the gate. And to make sure we
do not get their knowledge and wisdom for ourselves and act on our
own account they wrap it all up in Latin and mumbo-jumbo and pomp
and ceremony and forbid us even to read the holy Bible in our own
language, they *say* so that we shall not fall into error through
misunderstanding it but they *mean* so that we shall not find we have no
more use for them and their merchandise and give them notice to quit.
All this came on me suddenly one day like a bolt from the blue, though
I think it had been lying about in my head for a long time; and though
I've discussed it with myself and others many times since, nothing has
ever shaken me from it, and the books I read after that confirmed me
in it, not least the holy Bible itself when I got hold of it. Now there was
at that time living in Montereale a painter called Nicola, who came from
Porcia to do some paintings in the house of one de Lazzari, who was
married to the sister of the Don Ottavio who did his bit to get me into
prison, though not through anything Nicola told him, that I'd swear to,
unless it was something he let fall by accident concerning one of our
conversations. Since he found me of a questioning nature and was so
himself, though well-educated where I had hardly any education at all,
we struck up a friendship and used to drink and talk together. And
I put to him this discovery I had made about priests, expecting him to
knock it down with an argument I hadn't thought of. But he only smiled,
and said: 'But even if what you say is true, that the priests keep their

knowledge to themselves to keep their power, and only give us enough
so that we must rely on them, it does not follow from this that their
knowledge is false and the things they have us do are not necessary and
good.' I thought about this, and then I said: 'But even so, if a man tries
to persuade me to buy something, let us say a flock of sheep, and says,
"I think these look very fine sheep, you would do well to buy them",
and then I find he stands to make something out of the sheep being sold,
then I would look at what he was saying in a different light, thinking not
that he must be lying but simply that I must take a good look at the
sheep for myself and not take his word for it.' And he smiled again and
said: 'Then you'd better take a good look at the sheep, Menocchio.'
And he lent me some books, one of which was the ten stories of
Boccaccio in a forbidden book, that is to say the Holy Office had
forbidden some of the stories but the book I had was complete, and in
it I read one of the forbidden stories which is of the Three Rings.
In this story a great lord once declared his heir would be the one found
to have a certain ring of his; and when he drew near to dying he had
two other rings made, so like the one he had that no one could tell the
difference, and he gave one of the rings to each of his three sons, so that
each of the sons was sure he had the ring and inherited all the land, but
no one could know for sure, because the rings were so alike. And what
the story says is that in the same way God the Father has various
children whom He loves, such as Christians, Jews and Turks, and to each
of them He has given the will to live by his own law, and we do not know
which is the right one. This story I told them at my second trial, when it
came up that I'd said to someone that having been born a Christian
I wished to live as a Christian, but if I'd been born a Turk I should want
to live as a Turk. So I told them this story. And the holy father said,
'Do you then believe that we do not know which is the right law?' And
I said, 'Yes, I believe everyone believes he knows which is the right law,
Jews, Christians and Turks, because that is what they had from their
fathers and grandfathers, and that is why I want to remain a Christian.'
And that was the end of the matter, but I do not think I convinced them.
    And I had other books from other places, such as the Bible I already
spoke of. Once I bought a book, when I was in Venice, the *Fioretto
della Bibbia*, which I got for two soldi, and that was the book that made
me wonder if the Lord Jesus Christ really was born of a virgin or if it
was a priests' tale, because in the book, Joseph two or three times calls
Jesus his son, and it seemed to me to go against nature and against the
intellect that a virgin should have a child, and I think it was talking
about this that got up the nose of our priest Don Odorico Vorai, because
I didn't keep it to myself and this is why. It seems to me the desire a
man has to use his intellect is like the carnal desire, that is to say though
it comes to him privately and though he can satisfy it in a kind of way
by himself, the true satisfaction comes only by exchanging it with others,
which is what I did with my question about the Virgin Mary, putting it
first to the villagers, but they had nothing to say, except it was
blasphemy. So I told them what I thought about blasphemy not being

a sin. Then Domenico Melchiori said, 'Why should we argue with you? We've got priests to tell us what's right.' And I said, 'Yes, so that they can keep us under their thumbs and have a good time at our expense.' And he said, 'God has given us all our calling, me to be a shoemaker and you to be a miller, and a priest to talk about God.' And I said, 'And my calling is to blaspheme too, and that's what I shall do. But if your heads are too thick to discuss such things I'll go to Odorico Vorai and ask *him* about it.' Which I did, the next time I took confession, this was before I stopped going to him, and told him the thoughts I'd got into my head about the Virgin Mary, only to make it easier for us both I said perhaps it was the devil putting them there, and what did he think about it? Then he said he was quite sure it must be the devil putting them there and I must fight against them. And I said I was quite willing to do whatever he thought best, but I did not see how I could get rid of ideas which had come into my head unless I could prove them wrong, and that surely intellect did not come from the devil, and my intellect made it hard for me to understand how a virgin has a child. Whereupon Vorai grew very angry, and said the confessional was for confession not argument, and did I want to confess or not? And I said yes, I did. But that unless I was shown my error I was afraid the ideas would come back again as soon as I got home and I'd be back where I started. And he said, 'Then you are not truly penitent.' And I said, 'How can I be, if no one will prove my ideas wrong?' Then he said he could do nothing for me, and took me to see the Vicar General in Concordia, which was not what I expected, and when he got me there I was so scared I decided not to argue. The Vicar General, who I was to see again at my trial, told me my fanciful notions were heresies and I must not repeat them or measures would be taken, but must promise not to meddle with matters already decided by those wiser and holier than me, and this I promised. And after that I had no more dealings with Vorai but went for confession to Polcenigo, to Giovanni Melchiori, Domenico the shoemaker's cousin, whom I knew from childhood when we went to school together, there being a school in the district then. I knew Giovanni Melchiori, when he set his heart on being a priest, and now I remember a talk I had with him about that time, when I said, 'But, Giovanni, if you join the Church how will you be able to argue about things?' Because he was even worse than I was at arguing. And he said, 'When I'm a priest I shall know the truth and there'll be no need to argue.' And I said, 'How will you know it's the truth?' and he said, 'I shall have faith, and when you have faith all questions are answered, there'll be no more questions, and that's what I want.' Then I got angry and started to taunt him, I don't know why, and said all he really wanted to do was to sleep with nuns, and we had a fight. Yes, that was another time I wanted to hurt someone, because he had changed and drawn away from me, though the fact was, he was bigger than me and broke my nose, as you would see if you saw me since it never set straight so that all my life I only had to look in a glass to remember Giovanni Melchiori who tried to run away from his intellect.

But he never succeeded, because three or four years before my first trial, when he'd been many years a priest, he was up in front of the Inquisition for heresy. And his parishioners accused him of being a whoremonger and a ruffian, and treating the sacred things of the church without respect. But I'd heard before then that he was grown very careless with himself and drank a good deal and had mistresses in the village, which is not so unusual but he made no bones about it; and also that he was putting about the ideas of the Anabaptists. 'So,' I thought, 'Giovanni is arguing again. His faith has not done the trick after all.' But they let him off with a warning, and after my business with the Vicar General I went to see him for the first time in many years, and we grew to be friends again. Only a light had gone out of him. I mean that where he once argued as if he was at a feast, now it was more as if he was chewing on something unpleasant that he couldn't get out of his mouth. He was another one who said, when the Inquisition was looking into my case, that I should go straight to the Holy Office when I was called, because there was no escaping it, and said, 'Tell them what they want to know and no more, and don't argue, because they're not interested.' But the fact was they came for me before I had time to go to them, and took me away manacled. And as I have said, my mouth would not stay shut. And now I wish to write about that.

It was Friday, 2nd February when they took me to Concordia, and pouring with rain, and the year was 1584, so that I was then fifty-two years old. And on the Monday I was brought before the Inquisitor, Fra Montefalco. And to tell you how I felt, I had to evacuate twice before I went up there. Because I had in my head all the stories I'd heard about these trials and their results. So, I decided to be circumspect. I should say, my bowels decided for me. And at the end of the first day, when I was asked if I stood by the things the villagers said I'd said, I told the Inquisitor, 'Sir, I can't say whether all these things were inspired by God or the devil, and if they're true or false, for I'm ill-educated. But in future I'll follow only what is taught by the Lord God through the holy Church, and ask mercy for any errors I may have made.' And I went back to my cell feeling a little better, because it seemed a fair court and they listened closely to all I said and noted it all down and nodded.

And so it went on for two months or more, and I felt more and more at ease but tried to remember to watch my tongue. And to explain what happened then, I must go back to before my trial.

I wrote that the villagers had a way of grumbling at their lot, and it was often aimed at the nobles and the priests. But these grumbles did not come from nowhere. Many years ago — I had this from my father Giovanni Scandella, who was also a miller, and though he could neither read nor write he had an artful mind too — when my father was very young there was unrest in the region, which came from the nobles splitting into two sides, one side loyal to Venice and the other against it, so that the country people, infected by this unrest and seeing that the time was ripe, rose up and burnt a number of castles and killed

nobles, not bothering which side they were on since they were oppressed
by both; then this revolt was put down with great cruelty and slaughter
of peasants while the priests, always hand in glove with the nobles,
looked on. And as I said a man takes on the religion of his father and
grandfather, so he takes on their grievances too, and this is where the
grumbling comes from, though they know nothing of it, being like cage
birds that imitate human speech without knowing what it means. But to
me it meant a great deal, that some men could have dominion over
others and oppress them, and the priests seemed to me to be the worst
of all, since they not only oppress our bodies but our minds as well,
telling us what we can think and say and what we can't, living like fleas
on our backs that we pay with tithes for sucking our blood and if we cry
out at it they bite us again. It made me angry, and the village taking it all
as God's will made me angrier, and when I came to think even the things
the priests taught us were untrue, which was their only excuse for sitting
on our backs, you can understand why sometimes I shouted at the villagers
and wouldn't stop. It was this I had inside me at the trial, while I was being
humble and saying it must have been the devil in me, it was this I carried
about. But then they acted so quietly and reasonably, listening to what I
had to say and letting no evidence go by they thought might be untrue,
and Fra Montefalco dealt with me so kindly, in such a soft way, that my
fear went with my anger till I'd forgotten it was there. Then, toward the
end of April, 1584, which I remember because the sun was shining when
they took me up and all spring was out, two of the Fassetas were giving
evidence, yes, it was at the first trial it was said, I remember now, how I'd
told them that if I found myself ever in front of those who would listen,
be it pope or king or prince, I would say things to amaze them, and as for
the workings of the world, I had things to say on that too, if they killed
me afterwards. Then Fra Montefalco looked at me kindly, and said, 'Well,
now, Domenico Scandella, there is no pope, king or prince here, but say
what you have to say.' And he leaned back in his seat. Then I looked
round and caught the eye of the notary, waiting with his pen raised. And
I began to speak. And it was as if a book had been written inside my
head and I had only to read it over, if ever I felt the hand of God guiding
me it was then, and never before or since. I began by saying how the
poor were oppressed and tyrannised over by the rich, and how the
Church lent itself to this and took part in it and got fat on it, hiding
God's words from us where it says they should be as poor as we are and
live alongside us, hiding it all in Latin and hiding even the Gospels from
us where it says that when the Jews asked Jesus Christ what was the law
he said, 'Love God and your neighbour', which is all it comes to, all the
rest being mumbo-jumbo and merchandise put about by the priests to
keep themselves over us; and then I dealt with this merchandise: baptism,
because God blesses us when we are born and we don't need priests to
do it for us; and at the other end, extreme unction, because if a man has
sins when he dies God will know of it and perhaps forgive him, and he
won't be fooled by a priest pretending to make them disappear like a
conjuror at a fairground; and the marriage ceremony, because God did

not start marriage, man did, and if two people honestly make their
vows together and to God it was enough in olden times and is enough in
other places and should be enough for us; and the making of priests,
who pretend they know the tricks and charms to get us to Heaven
whereas all men are dear to God, Christians, heretics, Turks and Jews,
and will be saved by Him, and the priests only stand between us and Him
like clouds in front of the sun, and as for confession it is to God from
his heart that a man must confess, and if he is sincere he can do it as well
to a tree as to a priest. And so on. Only I said it better than this. And
when I'd emptied my head of it, they talked among themselves in low
voices, throwing glances at me, and I began to think I'd said more than
I should, but I could no more stop myself than stop breathing.

But my case went on two more weeks after that, because they wanted
to get back to the question of my ideas about how the world started and
where God came from and such matters, which I will write about later
on. And thinking I might as well be hanged for a sheep as a lamb, I
should say burnt — please God, let it not be the fire — I gave as good and
true an account of my ideas as I could, which is what I had always
wanted to do with learned people. But as I wrote, I got into tangles and
could have saved my breath. Then they went off to decide what to do
with me, which by then I knew could be nothing good. But I wrote a
letter to the Inquisitors in which I fell on my knees, you could say,
blaming my errors on a false spirit and asking forgiveness and mercy of
the most Holy Trinity, Father and Son and Holy Spirit, and the Glorious
Virgin Mary and all the saints in paradise and also of their most holy
and most reverend and most illustrious justices, and if I could have
thought of any other people I would have put them in too.

But as I have said, the sentence was that I stay in prison till I die,
which I nearly did, becoming so ill from the damp and foul air that I was
four months without getting off my bed, while my legs and face swelled
up and I nearly lost my hearing. Then at the beginning of the year 1586,
with ice on the earthen floor of my cell, my son Ziannuto sent me in a
lawyer and with his help I wrote a letter pleading for my release, the
contents of which I will not bother you with, except to say there was
no argument in it, only, you could say, a hand stretched out in
supplication. They had me up before them, where I fell on my face, not
in a manner of speech but in fact, and wept, I, Domenico Scandella, lay
on the floor in front of them and wept. As to what I said then, I
remember little of it and will not repeat what I do remember; except to
say that when I spoke then, from the floor, there was no choosing of
words on my part nor any holding back what I thought would be better
unsaid, but the words came out as if it had been blood bubbling out of
my mouth; and just as blood is of itself neither good nor bad, so the words
were neither true nor false but simply words bubbling out like blood.
And seeing that I was truly contrite they let me go, on the conditions
I told you about, that I stayed in my village, Montereale, and never spoke
again of my ideas, and wore always over my clothes the habitello with
the painted yellow cross to remind the world and myself of my sin.

I have written more than I wanted to, as I always spoke more than
I wanted to, more than was wise. And I have still not come to what
I want to say. But it will come, at the end. I must tell now of the time
after I came out of prison and before I came back in, which was thirteen
years.

Things did not go too badly for me after I came back to Montereale.
Ziannuto had taken over the two mills, and carried on with them, since
at first I was not strong enough to be much help and also it was better
if I kept in the background, with my habitello. And being a good worker
and a good business man, and popular in the district, Ziannuto did well,
and was able to look after both my family and his own, which he had
by that time. Only then Ziannuto died, and what he had passed to
his family, who wanted nothing to do with me. And the year after
that my wife died. And so I took to doing various things. I kept a
schoolroom where I taught children their abacus and to read and write,
which I thought important if others did not; and lent myself out as
sawyer or mason or carpenter, and was even an innkeeper for a while.
I knew by then that the Inquisition had its ears pricked for news of me
again, and I had not very much longer to wander free. I did think of
slipping away to Geneva or some other place men are allowed to think
and say what they like, but I was over sixty years old, and tired. So
I stayed, and waited for the blow to fall.

Because I still could not keep my mouth shut. When I came out,
I told myself I must not talk, I must keep my thoughts to myself, I must
act as other people do and say nothing that is not already known and
talked about. But then, we might be out in the night, perhaps on our
way back from the inn, and someone would say something about the
stars, and I would say — something, which came into my mind and
hopped out of my mouth before I could stop it. And there would be a
kind of shiver went out and they would say, 'But that's not what the
Church says about it.' And I would say, 'Well, then, I must be wrong.
What am I against the Church and all the world? I know nothing, pay no
attention to me.' But they remembered, and reported it when the time
came. And at other times, because I was still reading books and having
my thoughts, though I tried to keep them to myself, sometimes it was
as if, you could say, they boiled over and came rushing out like steam
and I'd say suddenly to someone, out of nothing, 'Do you know what
God is? He is everything, sky, earth, sea, air, abyss, hell, and us, we are
all God.' Or 'God is just a puff of air, that blows across us.' All this they
repeated, as I knew they would. But I couldn't help myself and even,
somehow, looked towards it. You'll say I was mad; maybe I was, and
am. We all carry necessities in ourselves, I think, and mine I suppose
was to think and blaspheme, and get caught for it, and think and
blaspheme again and be burnt for it, dear God make it easy for me.

So they took me, and I was in front of the Inquisitor again, a new
one this time. At the end of the first day of the trial I handed them a
letter, as I'd done the first time, calling myself an old man with worthless
fancies, and saying I wished I had died when I was young and saved

myself and others from the bother of my life; and that all I wanted to
think and believe was what was commanded of me. And I meant it from
my heart when I wrote it, because I was tired, and sick, of thinking and
of what came of it. And yet, even so, as the trial went on, I could not
stop myself arguing, I, Domenico Scandella, aged sixty-seven, I argued
my case. 'Listen, sir, I beg of you, listen to me,' I said, and 'But don't
you see . . . ?'

Then they gave their verdict, that I had slid back into heresy, and the
next month they said I should die for it. But before that they questioned
me under torture, as I wrote earlier, to find out my accomplices. First
they asked me, and I said I had talked to so many people I could not
remember them. Then they undressed and examined me, to see if I was
fit for torture, which I was, not having been long in prison. Then they
took me to the room, always asking the same question. Then they tied
me and prepared me for the *strappado*, asking all the time, and I said
I had it all from books and from my own head. Then they raised me up,
and asked again, and I said I knew no names, and then I said 'Let me
down and I'll think about it.' So they let me down and I pretended to
think and then said I could remember no one. Then they pulled me up
again and after a while I said 'Let me down and I'll say something.'
Then they let me down again and I gave them the name of Zuan
Francesco Montereale, the lord of our district, saying I'd spoken to him
about not knowing what the true faith was, and this seemed to satisfy
them. And though the next day I said Montereale had scolded me for
what I said to him, they did not hang me up anymore.

Now I can tell you of the idea that came to me since I have been in
here. At first, when sentence was passed and I knew I had nothing else
to do or hope for, I fell into a bad state, lying all day where I sleep —
I will not call it a bed — and nursing the ache in my shoulders, which still
was not so bad as the ache in my mind; hating the world, not just the
priests but the whole world that lets priests breed like flies on dung and
do what they do, and hating God for letting the world carry on in this
way when He was supposed to have sent His Son to redeem it and the
result of that was these priests, these dung-flies. And hating most of all
myself and what I was, a miller cursed with intellect and a mind that
wanted to know things beyond what I was told; and cursing my intellect
I cursed also my stupidity that made me think it was of value to the
world to be hungry for an understanding of things. So I stayed for
some weeks, in the darkest time of my life. But then, in spite of what
I will call my two winters, the one outside that I feel through these
walls, and the colder one inside, I, Domenico Scandella, who called
myself at this last trial, when they asked what I was, miller, mason,
carpenter, musician, teacher, philosopher, astrologer and prophet — and
I should have added 'buffoon', in spite of all, and in my own life's
winter too, I started to think again.

First I thought what I'd learned through bitter experience: that
these ideas and thoughts, that come into the mind like a miracle, glittering
like new coins, are not wanted in this world, only the old worn ones are

allowed, only those are taken as currency, that have been first through
a thousand pockets. Reading back over this I see I wrote of the priests
as hawks hovering above a field, where Menocchio crouches like a
fieldmouse. I will put it the other way about now, and say they are
mice, crawling with their bellies to the earth, and I have been the hawk.
Yes, I have flown and soared. And if this is vanity, then let it be, because
I believe it.

The next thing is harder, and came bit by bit as I sat here in my cell
day after day, thinking why am I here and what puts ideas into my head,
and why they should be forbidden, and I tried to think they did indeed
come from the devil, but I could not. Then I thought of a thing I had
argued with the Inquisitors, where I was telling them my idea of how the
world began and what made it, that in the beginning there was nothing
but a chaos where everything was mixed together and without form; and
as it swirled together there came out of its movement a mass of substance
just as cheese forms from milk, where the four elements, air, earth, fire
and water separated and took on their own properties. And within this
substance there came into being a kind of worms, just as worms form in
the cheese; and the most holy majesty, which is behind everything, made
these to be the angels, and the best and most perfect of them was God,
who was also created out of the mass at the same time. And just as a
baby when it comes first in the womb carries the man in it but is without
form or knowledge, until the parts separate and grow to fill the space, so
this intellect which was God when He was in the chaos did not know
Himself and had no knowledge, since there can be no knowledge without
things. And as the elements separated so He took knowledge from them,
and wanted to expand to fill the space and to go from imperfect to
perfect, and to do this He created the world, seas, sky, mountains, and
everything in it, and last of all mankind, using His angels as His skilled
workmen, so as to gain knowledge from it and fill it with His intellect.
But then the Inquisitor began to ask questions: whether God existed
before the chaos, and I said no, He was always in the chaos, and they
said what of this most holy majesty, and I said he existed from eternity,
even before the chaos, and they asked if the most holy majesty had made
God or who made Him and I said no one made Him but as the chaos
moves so He goes from imperfect to perfect, trying to fill the space, and
they said, and who moves the chaos, and I said it moves by itself! And I
was by that time completely muddled, and as for this most holy majesty
which I put behind and before everything, I do not know what I meant
by it. But now listen to me: if these ideas are true, or something like it,
then by another similitude we can say this: that a man's mind is like
another world, which starts as a chaos within his head; but then, as the
mind moves it falls into different parts and in these ideas and thoughts
and notions appear and grow as the worms do in the cheese or as the
angels and God Himself appeared in the mass that made the world; and
these ideas are as if they are live creatures and can move and do God's
work for Him and are part of God; so that it is God's work we do
when we think and when we have ideas we are acting as God, creating the

world and consuming it with intelligence, and we are being God. And this is why I say there are only two things we must do; one is to love our neighbour and not hurt him; and the other is to love God, which is creation. And there is one great error and sin, which all the world has fallen into and thinks a virtue, and this is to stop men's thought and punish them for their ideas and lock them up and burn them for using their intellect, because this is the sin of going against creation.

There is one last thing I thought as I was writing this: just as a whetstone will sharpen a blade, but if you use the whetstone wrongly or try to cut it you will blunt the blade; so, perhaps, these people are necessary and are part of God's purpose, these priests and such people, as whetstones against which we must try our thoughts. And perhaps the trials and troubles of this life are like the fire which anneals the blade. Because they also must be part of God's creation. But I have not thought properly about this, and now I am too tired to think any more. And if I had any purpose, I think it is done now. I ask your pardon for the length of this, and that I write as I talk, roughly and going from one thing to another like a dog sniffing at a hedge. And if I seem to be saying I know everything, I ask pardon for that too, since I know nothing and less than nothing. Even the words with which I began this, and with which I shall end it, I do not know if they have any value or truth in them or are only like charms the gypsies sell at fairs. Do with this what you think best, to show it to others or to light your fire with it. I must say now also that I do not know if the soul survives death, or what happens to it; but in case it does, I ask you to pray for mine.

In the name of the Father and of the Son and of the Holy Spirit. Amen.

HIROSHIMA: THE MOVIE

by Michael Wall

For Lizzie Slater

Michael Wall was born in Herefordshire, but moved to London in 1967. He wrote and directed a number of plays while reading English at the University of York. He never settled to any one job, although he has tried being a civil servant, a van driver, a grave digger and a sales assistant in Harrods. He has travelled extensively, especially in Europe and the Far East, and most of the material for his plays is drawn from his experiences abroad. He is particularly interested in Japan. His stage plays include *Japanese Style* (also a TV play) and *Blue Days*, and he has written many plays for radio. Until recently, he was playwright in residence at the Belgrade Theatre, Coventry.

Hiroshima: The Movie was first broadcast on BBC Radio 4 on 6 August 1985. The cast was as follows:

PAUL	Bill Paterson
SACHIKO	Megumi Shimanuki
BRUCE	Robin Summers
JAPANESE GIRL	Naoko Mori
COMMENTATOR SECOND AMERICAN }	Blain Fairman
JAPANESE VOICE TAKADA }	Togo Igawa
AMERICAN WOMAN PAUL'S MOTHER }	Gwen Cherrell
BRITISH POW AMERICAN MAN }	David Sinclair
JAPANESE KID	Kenjiro Hori
JAPANESE GIRL (non-speaking)	Midori Matsumoto
JAPANESE BOY (non-speaking)	Daisuke Shinoda

Director: Jeremy Mortimer
Running time, as broadcast: 57 minutes 57 seconds.

PAUL (*close*). Look.

The sound of a movie projector; then, an atom bomb explosion —
Hiroshima. The rumbling, with the sound of the projector, continues for
a long time.

    PAUL *is viewing the film. The rumbling and projector carry on*
through PAUL*'s monologue, but quieter.*

(*Close.*) I can't believe in what people call the real world. We look and
pass on. How does it survive when we're gone?

Street sounds fade into modern Japanese music (rock), and the sound of
young people dancing and laughing. The street sounds are still there,
underneath. The projector continues.

PAUL*'s voice is now heard in a different context; a street interview.*
The effects described above continue; all the sounds compete. There is
some confusion. PAUL struggles to make himself heard and understood.
He is a good interviewer. The scene becomes more dominant and the
projector less so as the scene progresses.

(*Off.*) Is there anyone here who speaks English? Anyone? English, yes?
You do?

JAPANESE GIRL (*approaching*). Yeah.

PAUL. Hi.

GIRL. Hi.

PAUL. So why are you dancing in Peace Park today?

GIRL. We always dance here.

PAUL. Are these your friends?

GIRL. Some of them.

PAUL. Why are you dancing?

GIRL. Why not?

PAUL. Do you live in Hiroshima?

GIRL. Yeah.

PAUL. Can I ask you questions about it?

GIRL. What, the city or the Bomb?

PAUL. The city.

GIRL. Okay.

PAUL. Do you like Peace Park?

GIRL. It's okay.

PAUL. Do you like the buildings they put up since the war?

GIRL. I don't know. I don't know what it was like before.

PAUL. There are a lot of office blocks, aren't there?

GIRL. Yeah, I like office blocks.

PAUL. You do?

GIRL. Yeah.

PAUL. Why do you like them?

GIRL. They're kinda restful. I want to have my own personal office
    block one day.

PAUL. What for?

GIRL. For dancing.

PAUL. You can't dance in an office block.

GIRL. Who says?

   The click of the projector snapping off.
   We are in a viewing room.

PAUL. 'Who says?'

   PAUL *has* BRUCE *with him.* BRUCE *is his assistant.* BRUCE
   usually sounds stoned. He is sorting film stock.

BRUCE. Smart kid.

PAUL. Yeah.

BRUCE. That's not a real interview, is it?

PAUL. How d'you mean?

BRUCE. Well, you scripted it, remember?

PAUL. So?

BRUCE. I don't know; it's your movie. I thought you were having no
    scripts, that's all.

PAUL. It was devised.

BRUCE. Yeah, that's what I mean. It's not strictly real then, is it?

PAUL. Did you see it?

BRUCE. Yeah, I *saw* it . . .

PAUL. Well, what is it you don't believe?

BRUCE. All I can say is, I hope you gave the kid something.

PAUL. Yes. She was better paid than any of us.

BRUCE. How much?

PAUL. She's in the movie.

    Cut.

Then, the atom bomb as before. It goes on, then gradually fades in behind the projector, as before, but softer now. No one speaks until the explosion is over. Then the AMERICAN COMMENTATOR *is heard on the piece of film. The soundtrack is slightly scratchy. Music plays behind the commentary.*

COMMENTATOR (*prerecorded*). Some of the casualties were horrific. Those at the epicentre were killed instantly. They were the lucky ones. But the heat from the giant fireball came at light speed and . . . (*continues.*)

BRUCE (*over the commentary*). You going to use this?

PAUL (*over*). I'm taking the voice off.

BRUCE (*over*). Good.

COMMENTATOR. . . . even before the blast hit began to roast people, melt glass, start numerous fires, char telegraph poles and burn the skin off people two miles away. This woman died soon after this film was taken. Remarkably this man survived. His skin was transformed into a huge heat-blister. Fifteen operations have partly restored his features, but his body bears living testimony to the power and potency of this deadly new weapon. His brother, who was working with him at the time was less fortunate: his skin was flayed from his body . . .

BRUCE (*over*). This colour's gonna match very badly.

COMMENTATOR. . . . the features of his face were blasted off and only his teeth remained. With his skin hanging over his pants like rags on a scarecrow he asked Ushio for water; then he collapsed . . .

    Cut.

PAUL (*close*). My film asks: why go to a place when you can see a movie of it?

    Then the commentary and the projector are back.

    (*To* BRUCE.) I don't want too much of this.

BRUCE. No, right. I'm just watching it. Phoo! Pretty powerful stuff, though. (*He winces.*) Oh, look at that. Jesus!

The film continues. They are silent. Then:

Oh, get a load of that. Fancy filming this though, Paul? Look at that face. God, couldn't they have done something else? I mean dropped it in the bloody sea or in the hills or something? This is bloody women and children.

Short pause.

PAUL (*to* BRUCE). We'll put the Mexico bit in here.

The projector stops.

BRUCE. What, here? Right after the face?

PAUL. Yeah.

BRUCE. Okay.

PAUL. So we go from — are you with me?

BRUCE. Yeah.

PAUL. We go from face to Mexican woman, to raft, North Africa, the women at the wedding.

BRUCE. Hang on . . . yeah . . .

PAUL. Then back to Sachiko.

BRUCE. Right. How much of Sachiko are we going to use?

PAUL. Good question.

BRUCE. Let's have a look.

BRUCE *is spooling the film.*
Cut.

PAUL (*close*). People blind from birth. What do they see when they dream? Anything at all? My mother is blind these days.

The sound of a clock ticking fades up.

(*Close.*) She can no longer see my films. She listens to the pictures and sees things that no one else sees.

MOTHER (*slightly distorted*). You were always a sad boy, Paul. Always talking about coming home and no sooner were you home than you were talking about going away again . . .

PAUL (*close*). 'Boy' — I was a man. Always with that guilt. Here with my moviola, here with my camera, my work permit, here with my ideas . . . Worlds in between — two, three, different people.

Oh, Sachiko . . .

A quiet bar background fades in.

SACHIKO. At least you have a mother.

PAUL. Oh, I have a mother all right. What do you mean?

SACHIKO. Not me. I don't have a mother.

PAUL. Everyone has a mother.

SACHIKO. But I don't know who she is.

PAUL. I see. Have you ever tried to find her?

SACHIKO. I tried.

PAUL. Don't you know anything about her?

SACHIKO. No.

PAUL. That's terrible. Who brought you up?

SACHIKO. My father.

PAUL. Well, how come . . . I mean how did you lose her?

SACHIKO. A lot of people got lost.

PAUL. What, you mean in the war?

SACHIKO. Never mind. Why do you make this kind of movie?

PAUL. I didn't always. I used to make other kinds of movies.

   Cut.

Thriller music.

   (*Close.*) There was a time when I made other kinds of films. I used to
   have assistants and second-units and makeup and continuity girls and
   gaffers. I used to get actors and dress them up. They arrived in the
   nick of time, they had emotional and marital and sexual problems.
   Sometimes they got the girl, sometimes they got what they deserved.
   I had an oeuvre, see? Then I got rid of the assistants and the second-
   units and I held my own camera. Get the picture? Nowadays they
   say I work with ideas; they say I'm an auteur. I've seen every movie
   that was ever made. I've seen everything. I'm heavily into irony.

The thriller music stops.

   Bit of irony? Here we go.

The atom bomb, as before.

   Tell me what sight in the world is more beautiful? Why do I love
   looking at it?

   Cut.

A Japanese street scene. PAUL *is talking to a* JAPANESE MAN. *The camera is running.*

So if you'd been standing here, say, where we're standing now, what would have been the first thing that might have happened to you?

JAPANESE MAN. Ah, first thing — your eyes finished.

PAUL. You'd go blind?

JAPANESE MAN. Yes, blind.

Cut.

PAUL *and* BRUCE *are in the viewing room. The projector is running, and we hear the* AMERICAN COMMENTATOR, *as before.*

COMMENTATOR. Hiroshima. They've rebuilt it now. Nothing is unbuilt in Japan, atom bomb or not. However, this city has not been rebuilt by men but by the Bomb itself. There is nothing beautiful or distinguished; there is only blandness and straight lines. 'Peace Park', 'Peace Boulevard', 'Peace Bank'. The new city is random, threadbare, short-term. It has been designed by the Bomb with new bombs in mind. When the next bomb comes there will be nothing to devastate. The job has already been done.

Short pause.

BRUCE. Except people, of course.

PAUL (*to* BRUCE). What?

BRUCE. Except people. They'll be devastated.

PAUL. Don't be glib.

Cut.

The sound of the interior of a tourist bus in Japan fades up.
SACHIKO *is speaking to the passengers over a small microphone.*

SACHIKO (*over the bus's loudspeaker*). We are now leaving Haiwa Odori and you can see on your right side the cenotaph where there is full list of all atomic bomb victims. On your left side is the new Hiroshima Hotel and ahead you can see already the famous Atomic Dome, which is ruins of the National Exhibition Centre and only one of few buildings still remaining from pre-war period. You can take good photographs now. We will enter Peace Park where we will disembark for your leisure and please do not be surprised if many young student approach you inside and ask please your opinion of A-bomb attack on Hiroshima. Please do not feel embarrassed, you can answer them frankly and without bad feeling . . .

Her voice continues inaudibly, under PAUL's.

PAUL (*close*). Why is Sachiko the centre of my film? Of course I do not suggest she *is* Japan; she is more than that. Close-up.

Her voice and all external sound stops.

(*Continued close.*) Her face. Her slightly turned-up nose, her pursed lips, her dimple, the one worry-line in her forehead. This is Sachiko. It couldn't be anyone else. Look. The breeze is stirring her hair through the open window of the bus. Her white glove holds the microphone. Her thoughts are moving, the camera is still. There is only Sachiko in the frame. She does not represent Japan, she substitutes herself for it. She will survive.

Cut.

The bar interior as before. SACHIKO *with* PAUL.

SACHIKO. I can't.

PAUL. Why not?

SACHIKO. I have my work.

PAUL. So take some leave. They'll give you some leave, surely, if you tell them it's for a film?

SACHIKO. I am tourist guide, not actress.

PAUL. I don't *want* you to be an actress.

SACHIKO. I don't know what kind of movie.

PAUL. It's all right; I just want to film you in various places in the city, all outdoors, okay? Don't worry — absolutely no hotel bedrooms.

SACHIKO (*laughs*). That is not my problem.

PAUL. What, then?

SACHIKO. Um . . . you see, I cannot help you. I am not free.

PAUL. What do you mean 'free'?

SACHIKO. It's not the right word, 'free'?

PAUL. Yes. Well, I don't know. It's a funny word.

SACHIKO. Free is *funny* word?

PAUL. No — look, never mind that. Why are you not 'free'?

SACHIKO. I have, um, duties.

PAUL. You mean your work?

SACHIKO. No not my work. Other kind of duties.

Pause.

You understand?

PAUL. No, not really.

SACHIKO. Ah, difficult to explain.

PAUL. I'm sorry, I know, it's hard, but it would be really nice to be able to use you . . .

SACHIKO. I want also. But . . . (*She stops.*)

PAUL. Surely we can get round these 'duties'. I mean we can operate on *your* schedule.

SACHIKO. My schedule, really?

PAUL. Of course. You're not a professional; we'll fit it in round you. Then you can go and perform your 'duties'.

SACHIKO (*smiles*). I think you already filmed me working.

PAUL. Yes we did.

SACHIKO. I thought — that guy's camera very big one. Also, you don't look so much like tourist.

PAUL. 'I just love your country.'

    Cut.

The projector again. PAUL's *voice is heard — a commentary on the film soundtrack. Behind it, lively Mexican music.*

PAUL (*on film*). I caught the night train back to the city. I didn't know what I was doing; I was running away from poverty, the film, and myself. I travelled first-class so I could have the breakfast.

    The music continues faintly and then disappears. We are in the viewing room. PAUL *and* SACHIKO *are watching the film.*
    The projector continues.

SACHIKO. You tricked me.

PAUL. Tricked you? Are you crazy? You're in a film.

    Pause.
    The sound of the projector and music.

SACHIKO. Your film is not about Japan.

PAUL. I never said it was.

SACHIKO. It is about other countries.

PAUL. There are a lot of countries out there.

SACHIKO. Why do you film in Hiroshima and now you show so many other places? (*Pause.*) I thought it was a movie about atomic bomb.

PAUL. Who says it isn't?

SACHIKO. I think this is Mexico. Nothing to do with atomic bomb.

PAUL. You've got to look.

SACHIKO. In Hiroshima there is no other story.

PAUL. Maybe.

SACHIKO. Definitely.

Pause.

Already it is somewhere else. Where is this?

PAUL. It's people on a raft. It's in Guatemala.

SACHIKO. I don't know this country.

PAUL. You do now.

SACHIKO. Simple people. No connection with atomic bomb.

Pause.

I don't understand your film.

PAUL *switches off the projector.*

PAUL. Do you understand James Bond films?

SACHIKO. Yes.

PAUL. That's good.

SACHIKO. James Bond movie is straightforward, honest.

PAUL. What's inside your head? Now? No, no. No thinking! Now?

SACHIKO. I don't know. Lots of things . . . Um, kind of jumbled up feelings.

PAUL. So what is it in my film you don't understand?

SACHIKO. In life there is story. (*Pause.*) You don't agree?

PAUL. Not particularly.

SACHIKO. I think so.

PAUL. Okay, what's yours?

SACHIKO. It is secret.

PAUL (*laughs*). There aren't any secrets. Don't you know *anything* about movies?

SACHIKO. Not so much.

PAUL. You should.

SACHIKO. Why?

PAUL. Because you live in Hiroshima.

Cut.

PAUL (*close*). I film Sachiko in a downtown bar. She wears a beige blouse with a black bow tie, black skirt just above the knee. Black shoes with red buckles.

Quieter now: a roadside Buddhist shrine.

She smells of the best perfume. I shoot her in parks, in coffee shops, in cable-cars, on castle ramparts, talking to friends. I film her at prayer. She stands before the enormous Buddha and claps her hands twice. She bows her head and the spirits come down. This does not show on film but can easily be imagined. Even in Hiroshima — of all places — you can do what Sachiko is doing here. Step off the street and find yourself at a shrine. You wash your hands with water from a wooden ladle, go up the steps to the Buddha, clap your hands and awaken the spirit. Anyone can do it, even a foreigner. The trains screech by overhead. I'd never noticed the shrines until I found Sachiko.

Cut.

SACHIKO (*close*). I had to do some terrible things to remain free. He has no idea. Even to reach my humble position in life. To say no. *No* husband, *no* children . . . Why do men want to humiliate you? Isn't it enough that you — do anything for them? Always there must be questions and follow-up. They want to take you over. Why must they humiliate you? What are they trying to remind you of?

A street scene, Japan. PAUL *is interviewing an* AMERICAN COUPLE. *The camera is running.*

AMERICAN MAN. Well we're familiar with all the, ah, arguments. I've heard 'em all and I've asked myself this question every day while we've been here and really, although, it was war and in war everything's, you know, kind of . . . well, let's say equally fair and unfair . . . still I can't help feeling, yeah, we could've given them a warning of some kind. Got the women and kids out, at least. They didn't have any retaliatory capability at that time. They'd've surrendered just the same. So I say yeah, we should've warned them.

PAUL. How about you?

WOMAN. Well I agree with my husband.

MAN. We agree on this. Just about the only damn thing we *do* agree on.

Cross fade on the sound of a passing car horn. Another AMERICAN MALE *with* PAUL. *He speaks differently from the last man.*

2ND AMERICAN. They should have had a warning, yeah. (*Pause.*) You been to the museum yet?

PAUL. No.

2ND AMERICAN. Oh, you should go. Really shattering. Make you see one thing: this must never, ever happen again. It's changed my outlook, I want to tell you.

PAUL. Didn't you know about all the injuries and things before you came here?

2ND AMERICAN. Yeah, but I'd never seen them at first hand like this.

PAUL. But this isn't first hand; it's a museum.

2ND AMERICAN. I know, but they've got a *movie* in there.

Cut to another interview. A quiet suburban garden. PAUL *with* TAKADA, *a Japanese man.*

PAUL. Is the atomic bomb the worst thing that's ever happened to your country?

TAKADA. Why you say it is worst thing?

PAUL. I'm asking you if you think it is.

TAKADA. Why you believe I think this?

PAUL. I don't know; just guessing.

TAKADA. Guessing? You must not guess, is very bad.

PAUL. Excuse me.

TAKADA. Of course atomic bomb is not worst thing for Japan.

PAUL. *Not* the worst?

TAKADA. Of course. Much worse is Black Ships.

PAUL. Black Ships? What are they?

TAKADA. Go and look in history books.

PAUL. You tell me.

TAKADA. No.

PAUL. Why won't you tell me?

TAKADA. Good experience for you, to look in book.

PAUL. I prefer movies.

TAKADA. You want movies but not books? This is not possible.

PAUL. Will you tell me what the Black Ships were?

TAKADA. No.

PAUL. Why not?

TAKADA. I don't want.

PAUL. Let's get this straight: the Black Ships were worse for Japan than the atomic bomb?

TAKADA. Yes, the Bomb is not so important. More dangerous, also, the Olympic Games in Tokyo.

PAUL. The Olympic Games were *dangerous*? Do I have to look in a book for that too?

TAKADA (*seriously*). No, you don't have to look in a book for that.

PAUL. Other countries have had the Olympic Games and they don't mind.

TAKADO. Exactly.

Cut.

SACHIKO (*close*). He wasn't serious. No Japanese talks that way about the Black Ships. He was teasing you.

Cut.

The projector. On film, Arab woman are shouting and wailing (Zaghrota).

BRUCE. That's nice. It's nice with the sun there. Are they whirling Dervishes?

PAUL. Shut up, Bruce.

Pause. The music continues.

BRUCE. By the way, I meant to ask you: you know that bit with the aircraft wing?

Short pause.

PAUL. Hmm?

BRUCE. You know where you just see the tip of the aircraft wing?

PAUL. What are you talking about?

BRUCE. Here, I'll show you . . .

The sound snaps off. The projector stops.
The sound of spooling.

You know the bit where the bomb drops, the aircraft turns away, right? It just catches the tip of the wing, doesn't it? The sun?

PAUL. What about it?

BRUCE. You want to keep it?

PAUL. Yes.

BRUCE. I thought you might; look.

The projector stops and starts. The atom bomb sequence.
Pause.

PAUL. It wasn't us that shot it.

BRUCE. No, we wouldn't have got the wing in shot, would we mate?

PAUL. You can let it run.

Pause. The Bomb is heard.

(*Quietly.*) Why do I like looking at it?

BRUCE. What? Yeah, it's beautiful isn't it? So long as you're not stood underneath the bloody thing. You know Sachiko asked me what your film was about?

PAUL. I thought she might. What did you tell her?

BRUCE. I told her about ninety-two minutes.

PAUL. She must have split her sides.

BRUCE. No, I told her it was a game, didn't I?

PAUL. A game? Thanks very much.

BRUCE. She asked me if I was happy to be working on it.

PAUL. You really had a chat didn't you?

BRUCE. I said I only liked games with balls and this film has no balls.

PAUL. She didn't get that, did she?

BRUCE. No.

Pause. The projector continues.

BRUCE. She's quite attractive really, isn't she? I like that little dimple-thing. Usually you only get kids with them.

PAUL. Are you stoned?

BRUCE. Naturally. Eh Paul? Where does she keep dashing off to? You notice how she keeps disappearing? You ever asked her?

PAUL. She's got a 'secret'.

BRUCE. Yeah? What is it?

PAUL. Are you kidding?

BRUCE. I thought we made movies and knew everything.

PAUL. Very satirical. She told me she's got a secret.

BRUCE. What did you say?

PAUL. I said that was nice; everyone should have one. She never knew her mother.

BRUCE. Is that it? Is that her secret?

PAUL. What's the matter, don't you like it?

BRUCE. I don't know; it doesn't sound like a thing to be, you know, especially secretive about. I know lots of people who never knew their mothers.

PAUL. All as stable and candid as you?

BRUCE. I mean, there we are doing a shot; she does it; we say 'ta love' and the next thing you know — phuit! — she's not there anymore. People usually tell you, don't they?

PAUL. I don't know.

BRUCE. Yeah, you know — 'sorry chaps, I've got to run, must catch the chemist before it closes' . . .

Cut.

PAUL (*close*). Bruce keeps on about this. Believing in nothing he believes in mystery. Why should I care where she goes to? What would it tell us about anything?

The projector.

Sachiko walking. By the sea. She looks left and right, she steps out. She has the natural performer's sense of where the camera is; she doesn't strain to avoid it; she isn't afraid to look straight back at it. I like that. She doesn't flinch. There is, you might say, more to her than meets the eye. The camera seeks this out. What does she look like when she's alone? Does she look different then? Maybe it would be worth following her. Always room for a rapid-tracking shot. After all, my film is open-ended, isn't it? Oblique, transitional, not James Bond. She looks away. Stop it there.

The projector stops.

She heard the sound of cut and she stopped. As we all do. She thought the camera had stopped filming, as we all would, but this day it hadn't. It was a trick. We kept filming. Here she is. Look at her. This is Sachiko . . . she is somewhere else. The mountains in the background, the sun on . . . but why am I telling you? Her face is turned away somewhat. Move in closer. Is this the real woman? Her face is — what would you say? — detached? Hard? Resentful? Private? Catch it and a chill passes through you. You can only do this on film.

Cut.

The interior of a room in Japan. PAUL *and* SACHIKO.

PAUL. Would it kill you to wear a kimono sometimes?

SACHIKO. What for?

PAUL. Because I want to film you wearing a kimono.

SACHIKO. We don't wear kimono these days.

PAUL. Who doesn't?

SACHIKO. Japanese women.

PAUL. I'm not talking about Japanese women; I'm talking about you.

SACHIKO. I'm tourist guide. Why would I wear kimono?

PAUL. You keep asking why all the time.

SACHIKO. I'm not actress, remember? You want an actress I can find one.

PAUL. I don't want an actress, I want you.

SACHIKO. I don't wear kimono.

PAUL. That's not the point.

SACHIKO. Go and get geisha.

PAUL. I don't want a geisha. How have I offended you?

SACHIKO. I never wear kimono.

PAUL. That's not the point.

SACHIKO. For me it is point.

PAUL (*reasonably*). You don't understand, Sachiko. I'm not interested in you.

SACHIKO. Ah, great!

PAUL. I didn't mean it like that.

SACHIKO. I know how you mean it.

PAUL. What I mean is — I'm making a film.

SACHIKO. You know nothing about me.

PAUL. Don't I?

SACHIKO. No.

PAUL. Okay, so tell me.

   Pause.

SACHIKO. You know nothing.

PAUL. Are you married? (*She laughs.*) What's funny?

SACHIKO. After so much time you ask me this.

PAUL. Well, you never asked me.

SACHIKO. I was married. Not any more.

PAUL. Ah well, shake. We do have something in common. I knew we did.

SACHIKO. You are not married?

PAUL. No, I make films.

SACHIKO. Films and religion. There is no difference for you.

PAUL. Yes there is. I don't believe in religion.

SACHIKO. Don't you want children?

PAUL. What for?

SACHIKO. All men want children.

PAUL. Do they? I don't understand that.

SACHIKO. To live after them.

PAUL. I'd rather my films did that. You understand, don't you? You don't *like* what I'm saying, but you understand. I can tell by the look on your face.

SACHIKO (*mock Japanese accent*). Japanese famous for having no expression on inscrutable oriental face.

PAUL. Tsk! Why couldn't you have said that on film?

SACHIKO. You only got to know me now, didn't you? When there is no camera.

PAUL. That's not true.

The sound of a bottle and glasses.

Here. Cheers!

SACHIKO. Cheers! (*They drink.*) Paul? Why do you make this kind of movie?

PAUL. What kind of movie?

SACHIKO. Kind of movie no one will see?

PAUL. Thanks very much.

SACHIKO. I'm sorry. Kind of cruel.

PAUL. I like being invited to festivals.

SACHIKO. You're a weird guy.

PAUL. I suppose you prefer guys who are more straightforward, like Bruce?

SACHIKO. Bruce? He's always stoned.

PAUL. It's a cry for help.

SACHIKO. You know he goes to prostitute.

PAUL. Does he?

SACHIKO. Didn't he tell you?

PAUL. Why should he tell me? He's my assistant, not my boyfriend.

SACHIKO. What do you talk about all the time?

PAUL. Films.

SACHIKO. Of course.

Pause.

PAUL. You know why I'm never bored? Because any time I want to I can take out a film and watch it; I know every single frame, every line.

SACHIKO. You mean on video?

PAUL. No, in my mind.

SACHIKO. Incredible memory.

PAUL. Yeah.

SACHIKO. But meanwhile there is real life.

PAUL. Who says?

SACHIKO. There is.

PAUL. Okay, prove it.

SACHIKO. I don't need to prove.

PAUL. Well all right. Tell me where it is you keep disappearing to.
(*Pause.*) Aha!

SACHIKO. I don't disappear.

PAUL. No, not to yourself you don't, but to us you do.

SACHIKO. What are you asking me?

PAUL. I don't know. I'm showing an interest in real life — or trying to.
This is what happens; it goes kind of quiet. But you work on the film;
we go all over Hiroshima, here, there, everywhere, then phuit! You
vanish.

SACHIKO. It is my right.

PAUL. Oh yeah, I'm not saying it isn't 'your right'.

SACHIKO. It is my business.

PAUL (*sighs*). Oh dear, see this is why I talk about films.

SACHIKO. I don't go anywhere!

Short pause.

PAUL. Okay. I'm sorry.

SACHIKO. Why do you ask me this?

PAUL. Look, I don't know. I don't care what you do.

SACHIKO. You know?

PAUL. What? (*He didn't hear.*)

SACHIKO. You follow me?

PAUL. Do I follow you? Christ, what do you think my name is —
Philip Marlowe?

SACHIKO. Ah!

PAUL. Hey look, I'm sorry. Come on, sit down. Come on.

SACHIKO. We stick to agreement, okay?

PAUL. Sure, yes, we'll stick to the agreement. Don't worry. Look,
I value your work enormously and I have absolutely no desire to . . .
investigate anything at all, okay? Don't nod, say yes.

SACHIKO. Yes.

Pause.

Ah, sorry! I must go!

PAUL. Oh . . .

SACHIKO. Sorry. Goodbye.

Cut.

Thriller music.

PAUL (*Bogart style*). She walked fast but she was a cinch to follow. Dame in a cherry-coloured vest and a short black skirt, like tailing a nun in a nudist colony. She left behind her a trail of oriental intrigue. I followed her to an alley; she threw a glance behind her. I dodged smartly into an open doorway. She walked on. She came to a green door set in the wall. She pressed a button and waited. A man answered the door; a few words were spoken. I heard them but I wasn't packing my dictionary. The man gave her a package. It was wrapped with green and red Mitsukoshi paper and tied with black string. She took the package and walked back in my direction.

Street sounds, slightly distorted.

(*Suddenly, to* SACHIKO.) Not so fast, lady!

SACHIKO (*slight echo*). Ah! So you followed me!

PAUL. Thought you were being smart, didn't you? What's in this pretty little package? Mitsukoshi, eh?

SACHIKO (*slight echo*). Can't you wait?

PAUL. Wait for what?

The viewing room.

BRUCE (*close*). Very clever inspector, but it doesn't alter the fact that she's going *somewhere*.

PAUL. I'm not trying to alter facts.

BRUCE. You've got an answer for everything, haven't you?

PAUL. I don't know.

Cut.

The projector. On film we hear PAUL *interviewing and English ex-prisoner of war. They are outside and there are three ex-POWs in the background.*

POW (*off*). Are you from the BBC?

PAUL (*off*). No, we're independent.

POW (*off*). Oh, I see — ITN.

PAUL (*slightly closer*). What are you doing here in Hiroshima?

POW (*off*). We were prisoners of war here when the thing went off.

PAUL (*off*). Really? Is this your first visit since?

POW (*off*). Yes. We're here for the anniversary, you know.

PAUL (*off*). How do you feel?

POW (*off*). Well . . . I must say they've done a magnificent job . . .

BRUCE (*over, in the viewing room*). You can't use this.

PAUL (*over, in the viewing room*). Shut up, Bruce.

POW (*continued*). . . . all this building and so on. If you'd seen it at the time you would never have believed it. You must have seen a film of it?

PAUL (*off*). Yes.

POW (*off*). Well, you'll have some idea then. It just goes to show what can be achieved if people put their minds to it. Some of these buildings, they're exact copies of the originals, so they tell me.

PAUL (*off*). Where was your camp?

POW (*off*). Outside of town, luckily. Over there about five miles.

PAUL (*off*). What were you doing when the bomb dropped?

POW (*off*). I was digging an air-raid shelter.

Laughter, muttering.

PAUL (*off*). What does he say?

POW (*off*). He says he was in the bog, that was the next best thing. (*Laughter.*) He says he dropped everything and ran! (*Laughter.*)

PAUL (*off*). You're very fortunate.

POW (*off*). Well this is it. It's all right us stood here laughing about it today, but it was no joke at the time, I can assure you. Of course we never realised how lucky we were. When you hear of these cases of lingering sickness, leukaemia and what have you. Yes, we were very lucky to have got out when we did.

PAUL (*off*). What would you do if another one fell out of the sky now?

POW (*off*). What would I do? Do you want a serious answer? I'd go and stand right underneath the bloody thing. That's the absolute gospel truth. I'd go and stand right underneath it.

Cut.

The sound of a woman singing. Japanese 'enka' music fades in.

PAUL (*close*). When I was a child I never cried except when I went to films. In the cinema I cried all the time. My mother liked films a lot too; she used to take me every week. But the trouble was we could

never get through an entire film because I'd become hysterical and
she'd have to take me out. I'm the only individual in the world
probably who burst into tears during Hans Christian Andersen starring
Danny Kaye. I remember the scene better than any from my so-called
real life childhood: Danny Kaye sitting by the sea singing to a group
of kids. One of the kids had what must have been a very short crew-
cut but I didn't know that. I thought he had no hair. Instant tears.
A boy with no hair! What terrible disease or catastrophe had caused
such a thing? My mother looked at me in disbelief . . .

The music fades slightly.

MOTHER (*slightly distorted*). Paul, it's only a film!

PAUL. 'Paul, it's only a film!' Only a film! What was she saying? Didn't
she realise how terrifying it was for me to see a boy with no hair?
What kind of a horrible world was she trying to keep from me?
Boys with no hair. I cried my eyes out.

Pause.

The sounds of a bar fade up. PAUL is writing.
The music is now being played in the bar.

BRUCE. She's gone.

PAUL. Hmm?

BRUCE. Sachiko's disappeared again. She didn't even say goodbye.

PAUL. Hm.

BRUCE. Can we afford another cup of coffee?

PAUL. I'm phoning New York tonight. We'll be getting that advance any
day now.

BRUCE. You think it might be enough to cover a cup of coffee?

PAUL. Yeah. But go easy on the cake.

BRUCE. Cake? If I wanted cake I wouldn't be with you. Dedication's a
wonderful thing, isn't it? What are you writing?

PAUL. Hang on.

PAUL. You see these waitresses?

BRUCE. Yeah.

PAUL. You see the short skirts they're wearing?

BRUCE. Well, I had noticed, yeah.

PAUL. Do you realise they've got no pants on underneath?

BRUCE. Really? How can you tell? Cor, I wish I was a film-maker, then
I might notice things like that.

PAUL. We're coming in here tomorrow and shooting this.

BRUCE. Nice light. Into waitresses with no pants now, are we? It's all right, I'm not making a moral whatsitsname; I'm just wondering, that's all.

PAUL. It's not what you think.

BRUCE. I know. It never is.

PAUL. Waitresses . . . Hiroshima . . . no pants . . . (*He stops.*)

BRUCE. It's a pleasure to watch you work, Boss. Looking for connections are we?

PAUL. Maybe. But it's not their *choice*, you see. It's the policy of the café. You want to work here, you have to wear no pants and bend over the customers. Who are the girls and why do they do it?

BRUCE. There must be a demand.

PAUL. There must be.

BRUCE. It's probably happening everywhere.

PAUL. I know. But I had to notice it in Hiroshima. And you see what the bar is called, Bruce?

BRUCE. No, I didn't notice.

PAUL. It's called the Hiroshima Bar.

BRUCE. Well, it's *in* Hiroshima. I don't know if that's . . . I'm probably on the wrong track as usual. But it's your film, isn't it? Personally I'm more interested in where she keeps disappearing to. I mean, let's get back to the *plot* here.

The music and bar fade to silence.

PAUL *and* SACHIKO *on a tram. The tram is stationary. The sound of distant traffic; Japanese voices; park sounds.*

PAUL (*coming-to*). Hmm.

SACHIKO. You were — what is that expression?

PAUL. Miles away.

SAKICHO. Miles away. Nice expression.

PAUL. Nicer than kilometres anyway.

SACHIKO. You were thinking about movies as usual?

PAUL. I was thinking about *Metropolis.*

SACHIKO. What's that?

PAUL. My God. Don't you know anything?

SACHIKO. I only see new films.

PAUL. What you see are old films; they *used* to make new films, when the industry was young.

A bell rings.

SACHIKO. It's starting.

The tram starts with a jolt and pulls away.

PAUL. Even the trams run on time.

SACHIKO. Only a short ride. We can get off at Eba Park and walk.

PAUL. Great, another park.

SACHIKO. You look naked without your camera.

PAUL. I bet you say that to all the tourists. I don't think I've ever seen a film set on a tram; I'll have to think.

SACHIKO. We are just passing the Betsui Temple.

PAUL (*flatly*). Lovely.

SACHIKO. Paul? Why do you make movies?

PAUL. Because it's the only thing you can do if you're interested in everything.

SACHIKO. I don't think you are interested in people.

PAUL. I didn't say I was interested in people.

SACHIKO. What do you see now?

PAUL. I see you.

SACHIKO. When you see me — you know me?

PAUL. Not without my camera.

SACHIKO. You see everything as a movie?

PAUL. Doesn't everybody?

SACHIKO. I don't like movies so much.

PAUL. It's not a question of liking.

SACHIKO. Paul? You are interested in everything, yes?

PAUL. Hm.

SAKICHO. Okay, I want to tell you a story.

PAUL. Some other time, Sachiko. I can never concentrate on stories. *The Third Man*, of *course*. There was a tram in that. Loads of Hungarian films. I've seen *lots* of tram films.

> *The sounds of the tram mixes into the rumble of the bomb. The projector and, on film, Japanese countryside fade in.*
> *The Bomb fades. The* POW *with* PAUL, *on film.*

POW. I looked up at the sky, I don't know why. I had my shirt off because I was digging and as I say I was stood in this bomb shelter they'd got me making. Anyway, I looked up and I saw these four parachutes floating down. I thought it was some sort of exercise; I didn't give it another thought. I got on with my work. I remember I didn't mind the job at all; it was good to have something to do. But if I hadn't looked away then, I didn't know this at the time, I'd've been blinded. Because three of those parachutes were carrying the signalling gear that was to set off the bomb which was coming down in the fourth parachute. I've always thought that's a funny way to drop a bomb, with a parachute, but of course it had to go off in mid-air. You know it went off right over a hospital; it was called the Shiwa Hospital. It was full of nurses and doctors and patients, and the whole lot just blew away. It wasn't a particularly loud bang; that's the funny part of it — you'd expect this enormous great wallop, wouldn't you? But it wasn't like that at all. It was just a sort of steady rumble, but it wasn't like any bomb I'd ever heard. Then, of course, there was the fireball, which I missed because by that time Charlie and I were underground, in this shelter. We were that lucky. Because people were blinded straight away, that looked at it, you know, and they were roasted if they were at all close to it. I remember, they came running up that hill over there, all their skin hanging off them and you couldn't make out their faces. A lot of them collapsed and died on the way up. They all had these terrible burns and blisters and they were all desperately trying to get something to drink. Except one old fella — he'd gone mad. He had a big piece of glass sticking out of his neck. There was nothing much we could do for any of them. That was the awful thing. Terrible.

Short pause.

PAUL. Do you dream about it much?

POW. Every night.

PAUL. Every night, really?

POW. In a manner of speaking. Because even if the dream happens to be about something entirely different — it's still there, you know. It's still very much present.

Short pause.

PAUL. What's your favourite movie?

POW. What's my favourite movie? Are you sure you're from ITN?

BRUCE (*over the film*). What did you say you were from ITN for?

POW. Let's see, I'll have to think about that one. You've taken me by surprise now. I haven't been for years. I don't know, anything with John Wayne in it. I enjoy a good cowboy.

BRUCE (*over the film*). Ooh . . . don't we all dear!

PAUL (*over the film*). Let's cut this.

BRUCE (*over the film*). Couldn't agree more.

The sound of the film stops. The sound of film being wound on.

The projector starts with a repeat of SACHIKO's *address to the tourists on the bus; this runs under the dialogue.*

PAUL. I think we've run out of things to look at here. I think it's time we got back to Tokyo.

BRUCE. I thought you wanted to shoot Sachiko in Miyajima?

PAUL. I've seen enough mountains. I need some low life.

BRUCE. What are we going to tell Sachiko?

PAUL. Tell her she's the best tourist guide we've ever worked with.

BRUCE. She took two weeks off; we've only used her for one. That's probably her annual holiday.

PAUL. Bruce, you got me all in tears. What are you suggesting I do? Spend a week shooting her with no film in the camera?

BRUCE. I don't know.

PAUL. You don't know, that's fantastic. We're making a *film* here and you tell me we're messing about a tourist guide.

BRUCE. No, it's just — we haven't used her properly. There's a lot we could do with Sachiko.

PAUL. Such as?

BRUCE. I don't know; you're the —

PAUL. Right. I'm the — What's the matter with you all of a sudden; we've been filming women all over the world . . .

BRUCE. I know . . .

PAUL. But Sachiko's special, is she?

BRUCE. I don't know, I suppose not.

PAUL. It's Sachiko and Hiroshima, right? A small part of the film. We've got character and setting. What we *don't* want is Sachiko full story and pics.

BRUCE. Okay, but we are shooting her tomorrow, aren't we?

PAUL. Yeah. I'm going back to the hotel.

BRUCE. Right.

PAUL. You coming?

BRUCE. I'm going to look around a bit.

PAUL. I'll see you then.

BRUCE. See you.

SACHIKO's *commentary fades.*

A park in Hiroshima.
PAUL *and* BRUCE *are filming* SACHIKO. *The camera is running.*

BRUCE. Okay love, just going to pin this on your lapel, okay?

SACHIKO. Okay. I don't know what you want me to say.

PAUL (*off*). Say anything.

SACHIKO. Hm?

PAUL (*slightly closer*). Say anything that comes into your head.

SACHIKO. What comes into my head is all Japanese.

PAUL. That's all right, speak Japanese.

SACHIKO. You want me to speak Japanese? What do you want me to say? (*To* BRUCE.) I don't know what he wants me to say.

PAUL. You're a tourist guide, you talk all the time.

SACHIKO. Yeah, but it's all prepared, that stuff.

PAUL. Tell us what you're wearing.

SACHIKO. The camera can see that.

PAUL. Jesus, tell us in Japanese.

SACHIKO (*in Japanese*). I am wearing a white blouse with a cherry-coloured waistcoat . . . (*In English.*) Oh, this is dumb! I'm not even an actress.

PAUL (*closer*). You're better than an actress.

SACHIKO. Oh man, you're . . .

PAUL. I'm not. I'm quite serious. You're beautiful.

SACHIKO. Oh come on, you're crazy.

PAUL. What do you see behind you?

SACHIKO. Nothing.

PAUL. Excellent. So turn round and look.

Short pause.

SACHIKO. I see the Atomic Dome, formerly the Industrial Exhibition Hall. Only place still standing from pre-war period.

PAUL. What do you feel when you look at it?

SACHIKO. Nothing.

PAUL. In Japanese, what do you feel?

Short pause.

What's the matter?

SACHIKO (*quietly*). I don't know.

PAUL. Is it possible to look around and feel love? Here? In Hiroshima?

SACHIKO. Love, I don't know.

PAUL. So tell me what you feel.

SACHIKO. I feel . . . (*In Japanese.*) lost. (*In English.*) That's what I feel. Lost.

PAUL. Cut.

> *The camera stops.*

That's very good, Sachiko.

SACHIKO. But we didn't start yet!

PAUL. We started ages ago.

SACHIKO. But I thought we were just testing and stuff. I didn't know you were filming.

PAUL. It was just what I wanted.

SACHIKO. But I didn't say anything. (*To* BRUCE.) Did I say anything?

BRUCE (*off*). Yes, you were good.

SACHIKO. This is incredible.

BRUCE. Paul doesn't make the usual kind of movie.

SACHIKO. No kidding. (*She goes off.*)

> Cut.

The sound of the viewing room.

BRUCE. I meant to tell you, I've found out one or two things about her . . .

PAUL (*close*). Not now, Bruce; I'm working. I don't know what to do about these kids.

> *A group of* JAPANESE SCHOOLCHILDREN. *They speak rough English, with strong American accents. Only one of them speaks, but the impression is of a group, with consultations and laughter and other responses.*

KID. Excuse me sir, may we ask you some questions?

BRUCE (*groans*). Oh no, they keep asking us this.

PAUL. What is it?

BRUCE. Oh, they keep asking us about the Bomb and all that. I don't know what they want us to do, burst into tears or what.

SACHIKO. It's for their school projects. They ask all the tourists.

PAUL. Okay, go on.

KID. What is your opinion of atomic bomb attack on Hiroshima?

PAUL. My opinion of the atomic bomb attack on Hiroshima is — that it was an excellent thing.

BRUCE. Oh, come on, Paul.

PAUL. A very *good* thing, understand?

KID. Good thing, really?

PAUL. It was a very good thing for the United States because it made the world safe for democracy and it was a very good thing for Japan because it taught them that there *is* such a thing as surrender. Everyone should learn this, even the Japanese.

BRUCE. They're recording this.

PAUL. I know.

The KIDS *are consulting.*

SACHIKO. They think you're being serious.

PAUL. They're smart kids. If they ask me again I'll give them a different answer.

SACHIKO. But they won't ask you again. They have recorded it.

PAUL. Well, that's their fault; they should have a camera, not a tape recorder, then they could see whether I'm serious or not.

SACHIKO. Why can't you just tell the truth?

The sounds fade. SACHIKO *proceeds to talk to the* KIDS *in Japanese. Her words run under* PAUL*'s monologue.*

PAUL (*close*). I'm a different person in every country I visit. Character is a reflex action upon one's surroundings, as subtle and responsive as a light-meter. Faced with injustice, misery, horror, I have acted frivolously. To behave frivolously in conditions of horror is the purest expression of freedom.

SACHIKO (*close*). Freedom. What about me?

The sound mixes into bar sounds (Japan).
BRUCE *and* PAUL *drinking.*

BRUCE. Paul?

PAUL. What?

BRUCE. Can I tell you now?

PAUL. Yeah, all right.

BRUCE. I've been speaking to Sachiko's friends, right? They don't know a thing about her. About where she goes to all the time. I asked them about it; you know they haven't got a clue? Yeah, they said, that is kind of strange, but that's as far as it went. Any time they ask her where she's been she just clams up, apparently.

PAUL. Well, it's her business, isn't it?

BRUCE. Yeah, but you're interested, aren't you?

PAUL. Well . . .

BRUCE. Because what I did was I followed her!

PAUL. You did, did you?

BRUCE. I just did it instinctively one time after we'd finished. She shot off, I was at a loose end, so . . .

PAUL. Very nice. Go on.

BRUCE. She went like the clappers. You could tell she wasn't like going *home*, it was one of her disappearing acts.

PAUL. Could you? I've met plenty of people who want to get home quickly. Some people even run to the launderette.

BRUCE. No, no. She had that sort of *set* look on her face, you know, when she's like really concentrating.

PAUL. This is fascinating.

BRUCE. Guess where I followed her, Paul.

PAUL. I give up.

BRUCE. I followed her to the hospital! (*He waits.*) That's where she goes, Paul. That's where she disappears to. The hospital.

PAUL. This is wonderful. Put this in a movie and no one would believe it.

BRUCE. She was carrying one of those little packages wrapped up in cloth that they carry.

PAUL. Get away. That's it, is it?

BRUCE. Well, it's more than you found out.

PAUL. I'm waiting to hear how it works out.

BRUCE. I couldn't follow her inside, could I?

PAUL. This is what you've been bursting to tell me?

BRUCE. What was I supposed to do? I don't like hospitals at the best of times, never mind Japanese ones.

PAUL. Well, this is absolutely riveting stuff. Japanese girl visits sick friend in hospital! No wonder I stick to documentary.

BRUCE. It's more than you found out.

PAUL. I wasn't trying to 'find out' anything.

BRUCE. It's more than you found out, and you're the one she likes.

PAUL. I think you should know — you're being irrelevant.

BRUCE. She'd tell you anything, man. I've seen the way she looks at you. She's longing for you to take an interest in her.

PAUL. You've been seeing too many movies.

BRUCE. What a bloody waste.

PAUL. What's the matter with you?

BRUCE. There's a story here, right under your nose, and you won't take it.

PAUL. I'm not looking for a 'story'. What am I, a newspaper man? Anyway, what do you want me to do, follow her all over town with a camera stuck in a plastic bag?

BRUCE. I'm not talking about the film. I'm talking about you as a . . . as a . . .

PAUL. As a human being sort of thing?

BRUCE. Yeah.

PAUL. Couldn't think of the word, could you? Why would I, even as a human being, want to know what she does in the hospital?

BRUCE. I agree, normally, so what? But because she's so secretive about it. Because she's so furtive and, damn it, because we're here and we're not in Birmingham.

PAUL. The bad women in Hitchcock are always blonde. You noticed that?

BRUCE. Please yourself.

PAUL. Let's go.

Cut.

The atom bomb, as before, but it cuts out suddenly as it is exploding.

PAUL (*close*). I woke up terrified. I couldn't tell if I'd been screaming or not. I'd been having a dream, but I couldn't remember it. Neither could I remember what country I was in. All I knew was it was dark and the curtains were stirring in the breeze. I was in Hiroshima and it was August and I'd made a film, part of a film, about a girl called Sachiko, and she was somewhere in the city. She worked as a tourist guide, she wore a black bow tie and cherry red waistcoats, she had pleasant friends, she was divorced, no children, and I knew nothing about her. I knew nothing out of *choice*, because what do you do when you know everything? What do you do when you're fulfilled? 'What do you want in life?' I asked the woman in California, just to get her to talk. 'To know myself' she said. It was a predictable reply. The film asked: 'Why do you want to know yourself? Are you suspicious?'

Cut. Silence.

SACHIKO (*close*). Why did I tell you?

PAUL (*close*). Because I'm a nice guy.

SACHIKO. Maybe you are.

PAUL (*smiling*). You didn't tell 'me'. You told the future.

SACHIKO. I don't care about the future.

　Cut.

External sounds: hills in Japan. PAUL *and* BRUCE *are filming* SACHIKO.

BRUCE. Amazing, what a view!

PAUL. There's no need to say that; we can see it's a nice view.

BRUCE. 'Just making conversation, mister.'

PAUL. Well don't.

BRUCE. Where d'you want her, with Hiroshima in the background?

PAUL. Yes, and the sea. Let's have plenty of sea. She's talking to camera okay?

BRUCE. What's she going to say this time?

PAUL. She'll think of something.

SACHIKO (*off*). Shall I sit here?

PAUL. All right. No, don't stop eating the ice-cream. You can eat the ice-cream. (*To* BRUCE.) She's a natural. Mike her, will you?

BRUCE. Will you say something please?

SACHIKO (*mike adjusting*). One, two, three . . .

PAUL. Okay. Bruce? Ready?

　The camera is running.

　Sachiko — this is our last session okay?

SACHIKO. Okay.

PAUL. Just say whatever comes into your head.

SACHIKO. Oh no, not again. I can't do this, Paul.

PAUL. It's because you always speak from a script; that's the trouble.

SACHIKO. English is a difficult language.

PAUL. Not really. There are five words for everything you want to say. You're spoilt for choice. That's freedom. Freedom to lie or tell the truth. Which are you telling, Sachiko?

SACHIKO. I'm not saying anything.

PAUL. You want me to help?

SACHIKO. Okay.

PAUL. You sure?

SACHIKO. Yeah.

PAUL. Why do you keep going to the hospital?

Short pause.

SACHIKO. Can you cut?

PAUL. No, we're not cutting. Why do you keep going to the hospital?

SACHIKO. I'm sorry, I want to cut.

PAUL. Stay there! You don't cut. We cut.

SACHIKO. How do you know about this?

PAUL. We're making a movie; we know everything.

SACHIKO. This isn't fair, Paul.

PAUL. Why? Who's in there?

SACHIKO. You really want to know?

PAUL. Of course. Film is very expensive.

SACHIKO. Do *you* want to know?

PAUL. Me? Not particularly.

SACHIKO. Nice guy.

PAUL. I scarcely make a living. Come on, tell us why.

SACHIKO. I go to the hospital — to visit my father. He has been there for ten years. Okay?

Short pause.

Is that okay?

PAUL. Okay for sound. Carry on.

SACHIKO. He was one of the Exposed Ones at the time of the Bomb. Do you know what that means, Exposed Ones? It means he was affected by radiation sickness, like many others. He didn't suffer at first, but in 1960 the doctors discovered incipient leukaemia. Pretty impressive I can tell you the name in English, isn't it? We learn the names of all the illnesses; we know them very well. Do you want me to continue? (*Pause.*) He is dying now, but it is very slow. I think he experiences pain. I go to see him as often as I can. I think soon he will die. This is real difficult to talk about. I never told anyone before. (*Pause.*) You made me tell you the truth.

Cut.

The sound of the atom bomb, as before, building up.

SACHIKO (*close*). I want to be loved for my face and for my body. Not for someone's 'idea' of me. My 'soul'. (*She laughs quietly.*) I want to be noticed, looked at. I want people to make way as I come towards them and I want to see my shadow on the ground. You are interested only in what I look like. Don't protest; I'm not insulted. I don't find it insulting. It makes me feel good. I can trust it. What I can't trust is your guilt. Please don't feel guilty anymore. I know how to live. We all do here.

The rumbling of the bomb slowly fades. The sound of the projector fades up. SACHIKO's voice is heard again, on the film.

You made me tell you the truth.

We are back in the studio, with PAUL and BRUCE. A match strikes. BRUCE is lighting up.

BRUCE. Amazing how they never cry, isn't it? Apparently they never cried at the time.

PAUL. At what time? (*Then:*) Oh, that time.

BRUCE. Not crying as we understand it.

PAUL. You 'understand' it?

BRUCE. They look as though they cry but they seem to do something else.

PAUL. Inscrutable to the finish. You think the film would work better if she cried?

BRUCE. I don't know. It's too late now, isn't it?

PAUL. We could always go back and belt her over the head.

BRUCE *laughs shortly.*

BRUCE. So that's it, is it? Sachiko's secret. It wasn't much, I agree, but it's quite nice there in the film. Funny thing to be secretive about, wasn't it? I mean, I know they're *different* and everything, but I didn't expect her to be like that really.

PAUL. What did you expect?

BRUCE. Well, I thought she'd be more modern sort of thing. But she was funny about things like that. Remember all the trouble you had getting her to put a kimono on? Bloody amateurs . . .

PAUL. It wasn't the whole story, Bruce.

BRUCE. What?

PAUL. The film doesn't tell the whole story.

Cut.

Interior. Distant music.
PAUL *and* SACHIKO.

PAUL. Here, this is for you — just a little 'arrigato' and thanks for all your help.

SACHIKO. Oh! But it's not necessary.

PAUL. Oh believe me, it's necessary. Go on, open it.

She unwraps the gift.

SACHIKO (*laughs*). Ah, I'm not surprised! *A History of the Movies.*
Is your name inside?

PAUL. Yes, here . . .

SACHIKO (*reading it*). Hm . . . it says here you are a wandering spirit,
a true independent. That's a beautiful expression.

PAUL. I'm not sure it's meant to be.

SACHIKO. Where will you go next?

PAUL. Well, we have to start thinking about finance again. Money.
New York, I think.

SACHIKO. 'Film is very expensive'.

PAUL. Yes. I'll let you have the details about the film, when it's going to
be shown and everything. Maybe you can come to a Festival showing.
In Delhi, maybe even Venice.

SACHIKO. That will be nice.

PAUL. I'll try and get you some expenses. I want you to see the film.

SACHIKO. I want to tell you a story. Very very short.

PAUL. Okay.

SACHIKO. Maybe not so boring for you.

PAUL. I won't be bored.

SACHIKO. It is surprising for me to tell you this. Because no other
person in the world knows. No one, do you understand? I told you
I visit my father in the hospital . . . Well, I didn't want to give
impression of very dutiful daughter. This is impression in your movie.
It is not true. I am not so dutiful. In fact, quite different. I do not
visit my father for loving reason. You remember I told you I do not
know who my mother is?

PAUL. I remember.

SACHIKO. He knows. But he doesn't tell me.

PAUL. He refuses?

SACHIKO. Yes, refuses.

PAUL. He won't tell you about your mother? Why not?

SACHIKO (*smiling*). It is difficult for you to understand, I think. He is
old-fashioned kind of Japanese. Maybe my mother was a low woman,
maybe prostitute. But there is great shame for my father. Many
times I have asked him — please tell me who is my mother? But every
time he refused. Even is she alive or dead?

PAUL. But he should tell you. You're not a kid.

SACHIKO. I know. I am determined he must tell me this before he dies. When he dies I can never find her. Maybe she's living here in Hiroshima, maybe even in your movie! He must tell me before he dies. I cannot love him because he will not tell me this.

PAUL. I see.

SACHIKO. Yes. Now you know everything.

PAUL. I don't know what to say. I'm sorry.

SACHIKO. No, no. Please, no sorry. (*Pause.*) I also have a present for you.

Rustling paper.

PAUL. For me? Oh no . . .

SACHIKO. Please . . .

PAUL *opens the package.*

SACHIKO. What's the matter?

PAUL. This paper.

SACHIKO. Yes. We always wrap presents in Japan.

PAUL (*his voice sounds different*). But it's Mitsukoshi . . .

SACHIKO. What is the matter?

PAUL. It's green and . . . red, and it's tied with black string.

SACHIKO (*laughs*). Yes. Special gift-wrapping. Go ahead, open it.

PAUL. Do you think I ought to?

SACHIKO. You are very suspicious. What do you think, it's a bomb?

PAUL. Well, all right.

SACHIKO. Please, open. Suspense!

Paper rustling again.

PAUL. It's beautiful.

SACHIKO. It is a man's kimono. It is very old, from Hiroshima.

PAUL. From Hiroshima?

SACHIKO. Yes. From long time ago, before the war, before everything. Some things were not destroyed, you see.

PAUL. Yes. It's beautiful. God, my silly present.

SACHIKO. No, you have been good to me.

PAUL. Good to you? You must be joking.

SACHIKO. But I am in your movie. You made me feel free.

PAUL. Sachiko — why did you tell me? Because I'm going away?

SACHIKO. Maybe. Maybe because you don't care. Usually everyone is
   — desperate to know everything, all your private business. You just
   wanted my face and to wear kimono. I like this very much.

PAUL. You make me feel very small.

SACHIKO. I don't mean to insult you.

PAUL. You don't insult me. You do me great honour.

   The sound fades.

The studio. PAUL *and* BRUCE.

PAUL (*close*). 'You do me great honour', I said.

BRUCE. What? Is that what you said to her?

PAUL. Yes.

BRUCE. Really?

PAUL. I just opened my mouth and there they were.

BRUCE. There what was?

PAUL. The words.

BRUCE. Oh. What did *she* say?

PAUL. She said *Sayonara*.

BRUCE. *Sayonara*. You know what that is translated? 'If so it must be.'

PAUL. Yeah? I thought it meant goodbye. Okay, let's see the Mexican
   bit.

   *The projector, followed by Mexican music (lively). The music
   continues . . .*